'Buy it. Read it. It is a memoir and a ~~~~~~~~~~ more than that. It is both broadly ~~~~~~~ political without a syllable of lazy thinking or labelling. An overdue reminder that class remains a defining component of identity. Funny and tragic, often in the same sentence. And perhaps most important of all, written with a clarity and beauty that leaves me breathless.'

Margaret Simons

'[Rick] writes brilliantly and bravely. He's a very talented person and [*One Hundred Years of Dirt*] is a really impressive piece of work.'

Leigh Sales

'A throat punch of a yarn that is as stark as it is stunning … Morton's self-awareness is breathtaking; his pain is palpable and his survival a triumph.'

Amanda Keenan

'*One Hundred Years of Dirt* has the sins of generations creeping down its spine. He takes you deep into an Australia you probably won't know about.'

Kathleen Noonan

'His honesty is both tender and dignified and is at painful odds with the drug-addled existence of his brother. His celebration of his mother is glorious … This is a gritty book whose writerly craft is determined to make something from dirt … It is inspiring to see a young writer (Morton is in his early thirties) lay down an emotionally complex story without any hint of affectation or pretence.'

Michael McGirr

'Morton is fresh. His book is brilliant, he's brilliant.'

Helen Elliott

'Incredible. I laughed and cried and punched the air often and all at once. The story explains Morton's brilliant insight into how poverty, class and trauma shape lives and how blind we are to their power.'

Sarah Macdonald

'From the Birdsville Roadhouse to the Higgs Field, with an emotional rollercoaster in between, this is a brutally raw, beautifully written, remarkably brave memoir.'

Simon Crerar

'This is a story as desolate and damaged as the land it begins on, but Morton brings it to life with compassion and transparency.'

Chloë Cooper

'I think this book should be read by every Australian.'

Stephen Romei

'This is a heartbreaking book about family breakdown and poverty. Rick Morton also delivers profound insights into Australian society ... It is a truly rewarding read.'

Michael Rowland

'*One Hundred Years of Dirt* is the universal story of the outsider, an unflinching memoir in which the mother is the unrewarded hero, and a testament to the strength of familial love and endurance.'

Euroa Gazette

'This is a book one does not speed through in stolen moments. It is a book one sets aside when there is time to savour the brilliance of the writing, to reflect on the subtle and not so subtle nuances of the narrative—it will be my gift to myself when I have the luxury of uninterrupted time.'

Fassifern Guardian

RICK MORTON

ONE HUNDRED YEARS OF DIRT

MELBOURNE
UNIVERSITY
PRESS

To my Earth mother, Deb.
I'm so lucky the universe gave me you.

MELBOURNE UNIVERSITY PRESS
An imprint of Melbourne University Publishing Limited
Level 1, 715 Swanston Street, Carlton, Victoria 3053, Australia
mup-contact@unimelb.edu.au
www.mup.com.au

First published 2018
Reprinted twice 2018
Text © Rick Morton, 2018
Design and typography © Melbourne University Publishing Limited, 2018

Cover design by John Canty
Typeset in Janson 11/17pt by Cannon Typesetting
Printed in Australia by McPherson's Printing Group

 A catalogue record for this book is available from the National Library of Australia

9780522873153 (paperback)
9780522873160 (ebook)

Contents

CHAPTER 1

THE HUNT

My sister Lauryn has taken up hunting wild pigs, which is a thing that people do. I have decided to join her and in our pre-hunt briefing she has not been able to guarantee my safety. 'You might end up in hospital but you're not going to die,' she says cheerily down the phone from her home in central Queensland. I fail to see how she can distinguish so clearly between the two options.

Later, she sends me photos of people who have been gored by boars. I think I can see the fat from inside their bodies. I am not entirely sure that is something that is meant to be visible, ordinarily. I'm thirty-one and have never knifed a pig.

Lauryn likes to impress upon me that I have gone 'soft' since leaving the cattle station she never had the chance to remember. She might be right. Station life was a medley of death—death was our life. It wasn't that we were brutal. Quite the opposite. Our mum Deb always told us that if an animal had a name, it couldn't be eaten.

There was a horse graveyard on the station where our father Rodney heaped the remains of the colts and geldings and mares who'd kicked the bucket, or in the case of my brother's tiny steed, rubbed up the wrong way against an old power pole. We devised a plan to supplement our income from the tooth fairy by prying the teeth from the skulls and leaving them under our pillows. The teeth being something in the order of ten times the size of our own, we figured we'd be rich. All we needed was a steady supply of dead ponies.

We did fill my turtle drum with too much water and my twin subjects climbed over the edge and died in the desert heat. They say a turtle carries its home with it, but unfortunately for mine, their houses did not come with running water.

No news is good news, which was doubly true when the weekly mail truck turned up and consigned our blue heeler Puppity to the benches of life. My other dog Tyson 'went for a walk' before disappearing completely, although I later discovered he had been shot because he was not a good working animal.

I rescued joeys from the pouches of their mothers after they had been culled—Dad again, with the rifle—and hung one in a pillow case beside my bed.

When a brown snake killed one of Mum's budgerigars, and she in turn applied the shovel, I retrieved the bird's stiff body the next morning and slammed it on the dining table while she was eating breakfast. 'You didn't bury him,' I scolded.

In hindsight, it had been a big night. The snake had made its way through a flyscreen window into the front room of our house and set about menacing the cockatoos, Bert and Ernie, and a fleet of budgies. Dad was away mustering with my older brother Toby when the snake upset mine and Mum's evening, and she was a terrible shot with the gun. The shovel was a grand idea until, in a fit of hysteria, Mum threw the shovel at the snake. We had lost our only weapon and the snake was now armed. After prolonging the skirmish, Mum eventually won the shovel back and finished the job, but we were emotionally exhausted and the room, which looked like a crime scene, was left for the morning.

That Mum was a bad shot did not mean she wasn't willing to use a gun in extreme situations. At dusk one evening when we were both in primary school, Toby and I thought it would be funny to do our best dingo howls 200 metres or so away from the homestead, behind the pig pens where we kept Sooty and Boris. The howls were too convincing and in the faint light of the dying day we saw Mum charge from the station house with a bolt-action rifle that she pointed right at us. We knew she couldn't see for quids, nor shoot straight. Our howls transformed into the pleas of small children in the line of fire and we were spared.

Dingoes, especially in times of searing drought, were a threat to our livelihood but it was the wild pigs that kept us busy. Wild pigs dig up root systems with their tusks and have resolutely destroyed the ecosystems in which they are found. They carry diseases, including worms that affect livestock, and they prey on small animals such as newborn lambs. Mostly we shot them, although my sister has upgraded her approach as an adult.

Lauryn goes out with teams of pig dogs fitted with GPS trackers. She tells me over the phone how her hunts usually go down: 'The dogs smell or hear the pigs and they go after 'em. And they bring 'em down by the ears and we go running after the dogs.'

So far, so good. Then Lauryn pauses for effect. 'You might have to run up to one kilometre.'

Cross-country was bad enough at school but there is this to be said for it: we weren't made to slaughter a wild animal at the end of the course. The Colosseum was big but nobody made the Romans run that far to knife a gladiator.

Because my sister's pursuit is somehow considered a sport, no guns are used. The killing is done at close range, with a knife. The trick, she says, is to approach the animal from behind after it has been pinned to the ground by the dogs. A person, me for instance, then grabs one of the hind legs to move it out of the way and, with their other hand, plunges the knife into the pig's heart.

Basic anatomy helps a little. 'You'll have to go between its ribs,' Lauryn says.

OK.

'And wriggle the knife around while it's inside.'

Yeah I'm going to stop you there, I say quietly to myself, without actually stopping her there. This is important, or something. I'm the country kid turned city slicker and Lauryn has gone full-blown country. If my sister needs me to physically and personally kill a pig to prove my credentials to her, I'm going to do it. Whole civilisations have been built on a similar premise. Why not a little brother–sister bonding?

'I'm just going to say it now,' she says. 'You will feel the blood run all over your hand.'

Goddamn it. 'I don't think I can do this,' I tell her.

'No shit! The worst part is the squealing.' What she means is the worst part *for me* is going to be the squealing, because she knows what I am like with pain and blood and the theatre of suffering. She loves it, which is why she became a midwife. That and also because this wild pig huntress is absolutely in love with bringing new life into the world. It's a beautiful contradiction.

Wild pigs are pests but I'm not one for killing any animal for the fun of it. Before I even started school I would go out with some men on the cattle station in the Toyota LandCruiser, with other men on bikes, and flush the pigs out of the bushes. There was no time for sport. In outback Queensland, where my family lays its scene, the unofficial manual on wild pigs is brief: shoot early and shoot often.

On one particular outing I was in the passenger seat and one of the jackaroos was driving when we separated a sow from its group. The jackaroo couldn't get a clear shot off with his rifle hanging out the window so instead he leaned on the accelerator and ran over the pig. There was a thud and the jackaroo turned to me and said, 'Don't tell your father.'

The boars, as it happens, can grow to LandCruiser-rattling sizes. A 130-kilogram monster was shot in western NSW in 2014. Others nudging 200 kilograms have been taken down in other parts of the country. To be perfectly clear, you really don't want to get anywhere near them. Certainly not on foot. 'The sows make a lot of noise,' Lauryn tells me. 'But the really scary things are the boars. You will never hear them coming because they are silent.'

Our excursion, on the 2018 Easter long weekend, turns out to be a fairly civilised affair. No pig dogs or a reliance on knives. Just thirty hunters with more shotguns and rifles than a mid-sized militia. When I step off the Greyhound bus in Dalby, west of the Great Dividing Range in Queensland, and meet my sister, who has driven down from Gladstone, I am still under the assumption we will be sleeping in a homestead on a friend of a friend's property, but this proves inaccurate. 'By the way, we're camping,' she says. The words are thrust at me. No tents, just swags by the river. I don't mind a swag but it's the mosquitoes that concern me. The river in question teems with Scotch Grey mozzies so big they can carry off small children.

A panic attack sets in on the two-hour drive to the property as I imagine all the ways I might be killed. It is likely, I figure, that I will be shot by some other hunter after being mistaken for a pig. Maybe I'll have an asthma attack on the back of the shooting buggy when it mows through grass seeds for the fifth hour straight. But neither fear is as great as my anxiety about the kind of people who go shooting. They—mostly men—are in possession of a rigorous masculinity. I haven't been ensconced in that world since I left the cattle station. Guns, Bundy and Coke, death. And me, the fay lost to Australia's urban environments, which is, in itself, cause for mistrust in the bush.

We're with Wendy and Drew, family friends, but it's the first time I have met Drew. Having learned I'm a journalist, he and his son Michael and his mate Tulloch soon take to calling me Paper Boy. Later, on our first night together, we discuss the Easter bunny.

'If he pokes his fucken head up I'll fucken shoot it,' Drew says to no-one in particular.

'He'll have no fucken head and kids'll be missin' out all over the joint,' another friend, John, offers.

The property is teeming with hares, feral cats, wild dogs and foxes, but we've come for the pigs. Trust a wild pig to make me realise how far I've come from my roots. On an earlier visit to Gladstone, I'd found a copy of *Babes & Boars* magazine in the passenger footwell of Lauryn's ute. I'd imagined how I felt was how parents feel when they discover their child has become a YouTube star, or a journalist. I'm seven years older than Lauryn and occasionally I have tried to act more like a father to her than a brother, but I saw then it had all been for nought. Part of me was proud this 23-year-old was still supporting the magazine industry, and publishing more broadly, but largely I was just confused. At least she hadn't submitted anything yet.

Lauryn and I are close, despite episodes of teasing in childhood ranging from periodic to sustained, but recently a clear gap has emerged. In Lauryn's mind, her gay, older brother is living the fancy life in Sydney's media scene, and in my view she is on the fast track to being featured in *Babes & Boars* and marrying a man based purely on how many pig dogs he owns. Both of these are gross stereotypes but such is the chasm between our cultural experiences.

In theory, we started out in the same place. For the first seven years of my life and the first three weeks of hers, it was a happy place. It was the sort of place where strange things happened, but as children we thought these things were almost magical, not odd at all. During the occasional big wet, we'd wake in our bedrooms and hear the sound of rushing water as the creek rose up and surrounded the homestead. When the droughts came, so did dust storms that would blot out the daytime sky.

When the weather permitted, we had visits from our very own Flying Nun, Sister Anne Maree Jensen, who'd learned to fly a plane in her late thirties so she could take over the Catholic Church's aerial ministry in outback Queensland. If the air was still, and it so often was, we'd hear the faint buzz of her Cessna before Sister Anne Maree radioed in with her call sign: Foxtrot Bravo Delta.

Outwardly, she didn't look like a nun at all, which was a touch disappointing. The Presentation sister wore jeans, a flanno shirt and work boots, so during my earliest years I thought Jesus was somehow affiliated with a long-haul trucking outfit. Just make the call and he delivers. Mum was Catholic but Sister Anne Maree wasn't much of the preachy sort, preferring instead to swing by for a chat and, when called on, help wrangle steers, muster, even pull beers behind the bar at the Birdsville Races.

Bush hawkers also dropped in by plane, to sell belts and hats, but they never took Toby and I for joy flights like Sister Anne Maree did. We never saw any angels on these aerial circuits but seeing the outback from the sky is really the only way to appreciate its totality. Of course, even from the air a person cannot fit it all in. You'd need to be bumping up against the edge of space to really cast your eye over it.

The Channel Country in far south-western Queensland is an arid floodplain, scarred by the capillary networks of Cooper Creek. The creek, brimming with yellowbelly fish, is fed by the Thomson and Barcoo rivers. There are four big rivers in the broader Queensland outback and these, alongside the Diamantina and Georgina systems, run for more than 1000 kilometres from the north and north-east into Lake Eyre, that great depression in the continent.

The people of the remote bush, like the water systems, also fall inward. By road, Brisbane is more than 200 kilometres closer to Melbourne than it is to Bedourie in Queensland's far west, where I was dragged along to dirt horse races as a kid. For the better part of the nineteenth century, these back-block reaches of interior Australia were, in practice, lawless. They produced people who have the kind of resistance to natural forces that aircraft engineers look for in testing.

A fabled 'Brisbane Line' was once supposed to have been drawn during World War II in case northern Australia needed to be abandoned to a Japanese invasion. Another, running longitudinally, might have been drawn by pastoralists to the west of the Great Dividing Range. The dingo barrier fence is probably more appropriate for demarcation, though. The dog fence runs through three states and at more than 5600 kilometres claims the honour of being the longest fence in the world. It also stands as a handy, man-made tribute to the priorities of those closer to civilisation. The design was clear: the fence would keep dingoes on one side in the largely empty interior and protect sheep flocks and graziers on the other side. There was just one small problem with the division: the interior was not entirely empty. We lived on that other side.

The continent itself hasn't been empty for 60 000 years and the land was charred and soaked with blood long before my gun-happy family took to it. The animals, even, have been shaped by hunting and brutality over the course of millennia. We might not have realised, but the violence that runs through our blood is more permanently written into the landscape itself.

There is little point arguing against the now well-regarded notion that Lauryn is tougher, funnier, more practical and determined than either my brother or me. In my family, we saved the best until last. Still, when Lauryn started her Bachelor of Midwifery in 2012, neither Mum nor I realised the strain that getting her across the finish line would place on all of us.

Lauryn's degree, through the University of Queensland, rightly demanded its students cope with an ever-increasing load of practical work placements, for which they would not be paid. The placements began each week in the first year but by the third, Lauryn was, for all intents and purposes, working as a midwife in a hospital without any pay. The key point here is that while she was doing these shifts, she was unable to work like any other university student to pay her way. On top of this, across the three years, Lauryn had to follow twenty women from pregnancy until after birth as part of her studies. She tracked them clinically and was on call at any hour of the day or night for when they gave birth; it didn't count if she missed the birth.

That's not to say my sister didn't work. When she wasn't studying or on call or on the ward, she did babysitting shifts in our country home town, or she pulled shifts at a local cafe, often after coming home from a night shift. To save money she did not move out of home, but this meant she had to drive the eighty minutes to uni and her placement each day, and pay $3 a day in parking.

Mum was still living on the poverty line herself, while I was just beginning to make decent money in my own career, though I was living in the nation's most expensive city. But between us, we cleared the way. Mum kept Lauryn housed and fed and I paid for sudden and insurmountable expenses as they came up: textbooks, bills, fuel, trips to the mechanic, car registration. In order to lift herself out of the socioeconomic bracket into which she had been born, my sister had to submit to a three-year trial of impoverishment while being overworked and under-rested. But it took three of us to get her out of there.

On our Easter pig hunt, I'm breathing in the tepid late-night air when Lauryn's gun goes off from the back of her HiLux. I continue wincing in anticipation of another gun shot. The paddocks are lit up with spotlights that tend to freeze our prey long enough for someone to get off a shot.

Late in the evening we latch on to a swarm of pigs in the long grass and give chase. Mostly we are just chasing after indentations in the grass itself, which is as tall as a man in parts. Then a pig materialises about a metre in front of the HiLux and shots ring out in the night. The animal can zig-zag for Australia. Everyone misses.

Lauryn's midwife friend Tash and her mate Michael, a para-medic, have joined us for the weekend. Michael brings four guns, including a .308 rifle, a .223 and an Adler 12G shotgun. The latter kicks so hard when I fire it that I am thrown back to childhood and memories of all the dead arms Toby playfully gave me.

We only kill one pig. One of the men runs over it in a buggy and leaps out to knife it in the heart so it dies quickly. The next day we return to find that the pig, just a small one, is missing its head and tail. My sister picks it up by a hoof and hands it to me, demanding I hold it. The only squeals I hear that weekend are her shrieks of excitement as I pose for a photo with what is left of the poor thing. Drew calls out: 'Breaking news. Journalist gnaws head off fucken pig.' Everyone laughs.

The single experience of my sister's road to this point detonates the argument that equality of opportunity is stitched into our nationhood. Lauryn was forced to work harder and smarter, not just at university but around it, to get her degree. There are others who would have worked even harder than her, and plenty more who tried and couldn't make it.

Unlike me, Lauryn still sees much of that world in the work she does. That she now shoots pigs for fun is reward for effort. After working as hard as she did, as we all did, who doesn't want to blow off a little steam, or even, as the case may be, a wild boar?

CHAPTER 2

NOTHING AND EVERYTHING

In the beginning, my family owned 0.4 per cent of the entire Australian landmass. This is quite a lot. Indeed, it is very big. My grandfather, George Morton, and his family possessed five cattle stations collectively the size of Belgium—30 000 square kilometres— in the kind of country known for killing lost European tourists. The flagship was Pandie Pandie Station, 6625 square kilometres of stony claypan just south of the Queensland–South Australia border, off the Birdsville Track.

It took a particular type of person to live there. The landscape was vicious and largely incompatible with life. During the violent dust storms that brewed in the Simpson Desert, 100 kilometres to the west of Pandie Pandie, the tops of sand dunes, themselves 30 metres high, would be whipped off and carted east. Life stopped when these storms swept in, dumping sand through every opening in the homestead. The wind moved the desert indoors and it would need to be taken out again, not by dustpan and broom but with shovel and wheelbarrow.

'There are stories of weak, thirsty cattle being covered where they lay, of stockmen lost between cattle yards and the dinner camp,' local historian Lois Litchfield writes in her book on the region, *Marree and the Tracks Beyond*. 'The devastating sensation of checking a sleeping baby in his cot, only to find him completely covered with sand, ears and eye sockets full, as though he'd been there for months rather than minutes.'

Here, on these torrid plains, my grandfather began one of Australia's longest-running border disputes with his neighbour Lyle, who also happened to be his brother. What follows is fortunately the subject of newspaper record, else it could scarcely be believed.

The year is 1973 and Lyle Morton, a sensible man, apparently agreed with my grandfather to build a boundary fence, which ran the 40 kilometres between their two stations, Roseberth and Pandie Pandie. The stations had once been a single sprawling behemoth but were now being run separately. Lyle's estimation of the subsequent falling out, in the pages of *The Australian* in 2002, was precise: 'He wouldn't pay for his half of the fucken fence.' The punch-on that followed at the Birdsville Hotel is still the stuff of local legend.

Here, however, the story enters bizarre territory. According to Lyle, the once-in-a-generation floods that swept Queensland in 1974 knocked out the boundary fence. 'So I told the fucken bastard it was his turn to build another one,' he told the newspaper. 'He refused, so I built me own fence, [200 metres] away from the boundary. To get back at me, the fucken bastard built his own fence along the boundary. The area in between is no-man's land.'

Lyle fleshed out the story when he told it again in 2008 to *The Courier-Mail*. 'When the cattle walked up to the fence they were on Roseberth so I used to put them on my side of the fence and then straight to the cool room,' he said. 'But George caught on and decided to put his own fence up and there were two fences.'

The 'demilitarised zone' as Lyle called it—all 12 square kilometres of it—remained until my grandfather's death more than thirty years later. Both fences are still standing today, maintained by my father's cousin on one side and my cousin on the other.

When last quizzed about this extraordinary act of intransigence, almost three decades after the argument began, my grandfather wasted little time on it. 'It's that bloody stupid I don't want to talk about it. He's [Lyle's] as silly as a fucken wheel,' George told *The Australian*. 'There was never any fucken problem. He was just adamant that he wanted to put up another fence. There was no fucken problem.'

When I run into Geoff Morton, Lyle's son, at the Birdsville Roadhouse, I ask him about the matter. 'The whole thing was never put up to be a dispute,' he says, before stopping himself. 'Well, it was a dispute. The original fence, they were all running one show at the one time, the two brothers on either side.' The key, he goes on to say, was how cattle moved.

'In this country, everywhere in this country you see, cattle always go south. Ninety-nine days out of 100 they will always go south,' Geoff says. 'So anyway the first flood comes and knocks down this new fence and Roseberth had to put it up again because we're north, you see, so we had to have the fence. Every year it was just a run of seasons, one after the other, so after about three or four of knocking them [fences] down Lyle said, "Your turn George to put it up". And course he knew he didn't have to, so he sweated it out thinking it would just go back up again. And it did, but over here.'

And then Lyle waited for that one time in 100 when the cattle moved north. And when they did, he pounced. 'So of course when that happened all the Roseberth ringers went along the line,' says Geoff, who makes a whooshing sound before adding, 'and took everything. We did it about three times and the next thing there was a fence up.'

In a country known for hardship in the face of natural forces, even familial ones, there is almost nowhere more difficult to live than on the Birdsville Track. It will wring the life out of you and has been doing so for tens of thousands of years.

In the 1960s a family of five English migrants travelled by car along this gibber track, striking north for a new life from the former railway town of Marree. It was the Christmas holidays, summer, and nobody knew they were trying to get to Queensland. The Page family took a wrong turn in the night, damaged the gearbox on those smooth gibber stones, and ran out of fuel on Christmas Eve, 60 kilometres south-west of George Morton's station.

Few people travel this expanse of nothing, even during peak season. But this was the day before Christmas. There was no mail run, no food run, and other families had already travelled south or north to be with those they loved. And in any case, the Pages were not on the Birdsville Track. No-one was coming for them.

It was my grandfather who found their bodies. I try to imagine what that must have been like, scanning the emptiness of that space from his neighbour's station aircraft. George found three of them under a coolabah tree. One of the little ones had paced around in circles not far away, eventually falling in the 50-degree heat. The oldest son was found the next day. He had climbed Deadman's Sandhill and tied his shirt to a gidgee tree, still trying to get help.

My father Rodney was three-and-a-half years old when the bodies were found, and though I imagine he was too young to remember it, I have caught myself wondering whether his father came home any different that day. Was he as violent and cruel as he was going to get, or did it get worse?

George Villiers Morton was a hefty and intimidating man. He had those Morton bones, as if they had been petrified first before the flesh was sewn on. He owned every room he ever walked into and seldom had to enforce the terms of his own presence.

The Mortons had been on the Birdsville Track since the turn of the century. It was theirs. A plausible explanation for the colony's failure to launch a carbon copy of class as it was once known on milder shores is that great, yawning interior of the Australian continent and a distinct lack of hands. The need to survive required mutation. There was work to be done and free landholders couldn't afford to sit back and issue orders from the sidelines. These typically highborn squatters became, in effect, Australia's landed gentry but with a much more practical flourish. It was into such a family, quite some time later, that I was born.

In a way, we were caught between the inherited mistakes of the Empire. Our cattle station, like many others, was overrun by introduced species, and my father's idea of himself was tangled up in the need to have his own vast property. But solving the problem of the Morton family's diminishing status was not that simple. Rodney was the second-youngest of seven children and competed admirably for the position of least favourite. Despite his parents owning sprawling pastoral titles across four states and territories, there would be no property held for him.

In far west Queensland, near the border with South Australia, you will find Mount Howitt Station, the last property Rodney Morton managed before our worlds divided. Mount Howitt was 100000 hectares of beef cattle country but Rodney always found it a bit small. To him, it was embarrassing. Mount Howitt was owned by the then Stanbroke Pastoral Company. My father simply managed it.

Here, on our patch of dirt, little of the normal world crept in. We lived fourteen hours' drive west of Brisbane, sixteen hours north-west of Sydney and the same distance by road north-east of Adelaide. Canberra was fifteen hours away but to us it might have been another universe. Still, this property was dwarfed in scale by the Morton family pastoral leases. Big meant powerful.

Mum tells me that George would hold court, like a mafia boss, at the Birdsville Races each year. There he would be, solid and immoveable at his table, and the cattlemen would come to him for counsel. He never moved but the guests cycled through.

George was king of both the cattlemen and his environment in a vast complex of fear. That is, above all else, what the outback can install in the uninitiated. Fear of the weather, fear of the beasts, fear that if something goes truly, terribly wrong, those distances are so great, so unreachable, that hope becomes a nebulous term.

Then there is, of course, the not insignificant matter of what those astonishing distances do to the very idea of right and wrong. They bend light around the truth, as my family would discover. Manage, even, to erase it. Ghastly things can happen out here and, at precisely the same time, never have happened at all.

My father was five when his own dad threw him into a wall and ruptured his spleen. He was sent, alone and afraid, to Adelaide, 1100 kilometres away, where he had emergency surgery.

The only thing more constant than the physical blows to the head my grandfather meted out as punishment were the vitriol and emotional subterfuge. Rodney was not George's son; he was useless, a sissy. If my grandfather ever told my dad he was loved, they were words rendered meaningless by his actions.

There were six other children, my paternal uncles and aunts, and the family politics revolved around life on the land. All of them, save for the eldest daughter, expected to run their own stations one day and George held this ideal in front of them as future reward for current loyalty. He ruled by fear. A Supreme Court judge found as much during a legal battle for one such station at the end of the 1990s.

Craig Morton, my uncle, was to marry and had decided he could not live with his new bride on Pandie Pandie, the seat of Morton power in the west and the undisputed domain of my grandfather. At his wedding, however, George made him an offer, which has been recorded in evidence at the Supreme Court of South Australia. 'You can come home but we've got no work to do,' George told him. 'If I get another place, you can go down and look after it.' My grandfather did buy that property, 40 000 hectares of sheep country 176 kilometres east of Broken Hill in the NSW outback, purchased for $620 000. Barraroo would, in time, be Craig's. He just had to run it until the property made a profit.

In 1982, Craig and his wife Jacqueline moved to Barraroo and began running the station on a meagre wage. Seven years later, it made money and Craig raised the formal partnership he had with my grandfather. George's response was characteristic in its brevity and anger. 'He told me I wouldn't fucking know what I was fucking talking about,' Craig told the court.

As part of the partnership, the stock provided to Barraroo and another station George subsequently bought for his daughter Rainie was recorded as a shared asset. The judge also noted George's behaviour on this front: 'However, in a confused way, no doubt a reflection of the autocratic fashion in which Mr George Morton dealt with the operating of the partnership, he clung to the idea that the stock, at least the cattle, and possibly the sheep, still belonged to him.'

Autocratic. Here, to a distant outsider, was the word that best summed up my grandfather. He was a despot, well fed and enraged like the best of them, and never challenged. He made overtures and vague promises when he needed to, but in the end, his kingdom was built on terror. George Morton's subjects were not civilians in a far-flung country but his own children. In the middle of nowhere, but in Australia.

This legal challenge sent ripples through the family. Some forty years after Craig had been born, and almost five decades since the eldest arrived, one of George Morton's children had stood up to him. That Craig did it in a court of law worked better, it turned out, than my father's own attempt at justice. Rodney tried to stab his father with a screwdriver. As revolutions go, it was short-lived.

I recalled this case because the judge made another remark that sets in time and space the nature of my family's beginnings and gives contour to the struggles of the generations that would follow. On discussion of a point of law, the judge ruled that using the actual legal definitions of words would be of no use to the case. 'These people are not particularly well educated; they are certainly not lawyers; they are not used to, because they have no need, expressing themselves precisely,' he said.

The way the Morton children, my father included, came to get any education at all was by my long-suffering grandmother Lorrie, George's wife. She made a Faustian pact with her husband during the only moment in their marriage when she had undeniable leverage over him. The details have eroded over the years but we know George had assaulted an Aboriginal woman, perhaps even raped her, and was facing the consequences of his predatory behaviour. The only alibi he could conceivably employ was Lorrie, who knew she was not with him on the night in question. Here, in the fires of a mother's imperfect hierarchy, she made a pitch to save her husband in return for the education of her children.

To understand the import of this bargain, one must fully understand the geography of George's dominion. Pandie Pandie Station was a prison. The memorial stone for the Page family serves as a reminder of this, cruel and clear. You get out of the desolate landscape only if you have the means. A working vehicle, fuel and the know-how are a must. George saw both his properties and his children as chess pieces in a game of strategy, but they were his only as long as he controlled them. He knew if the fear of his wrath didn't keep them in deference to his wishes, then the sheer physics of their home country would at least prevent them escaping.

While George and Lorrie went to the wedding of one son, George made three children stay behind on the property to run it in his absence. All three, my father included, knew they were on a hiding to nothing. George would return and no matter what had transpired he would be angry and in need of reasserting his control. If the teenaged Morton children had found an extra 1000 head of cattle and convinced the beasts to truck and subsequently slaughter themselves, it would not have been enough.

Graham, the eldest of the three left behind, saw the writing on the wall. As soon as his father had left, he turned to his brothers and announced he was getting out of there. 'Fuck this,' he said to them one day when they were in Birdsville. He never went back to Pandie Pandie and never worked for his father again. He had left the family and so was declared persona non grata.

By the time George Morton was accused of assault, my father was becoming a teenager. He had not done any formal schooling and had been worked from the moment he could walk. Lorrie's bargain, morally reprehensible as it was, landed my dad two years of boarding school in Adelaide.

Lorrie's story is the most complex of them all. Born an Oldfield, her roots in the area went back generations to a Scottish migrant, Alexander Scobie, who settled on the Birdsville Track some time around 1880. When the pioneering Scobie sunk a well 8 kilometres south of the current Cowarie Station, he moved his wife Mary and their then three children onto the land. The first homestead they built was made of cane grass and had no windows. Undeterred, Mary hung curtains where she thought windows ought to have been, which I think says a lot about the kind of mutilated optimism one needs to get by out there.

The hottest official temperature ever recorded in Australia was in 1960 at Oodnadatta, on the other side of the Simpson Desert, at 50.7 degrees. Locals will tell you it gets hotter, of course, but it is safe to say Alexander and Mary suffered in those heavy summers.

Three generations later, Lorrie was raised on the same station, which had become bigger and, on account of the goats Mary Clarke had introduced for milk decades earlier, infested with the hoofed animals. According to Lois Litchfield, the goats would invade the rundown homestead en masse at the first sign of rain. 'There's a heap of bones that bears testimony to the desperate measures that eventually had to be taken to regain control of the house,' she writes.

Litchfield takes this morsel away as quickly as it is offered. Unfortunately, there is no further explanation of the 'desperate measures' taken. In the absence of clarifying information, a whole universe of possibilities opens up. Was there a last stand of the goats of some description? An extinction event? We shall never know.

In any event, this was Lorrie's home and when she came of age she married George, in 1950. I'm not sure how much love ever entered the equation. That veiny patch of Australia known as the Channel Country was her only home. The Morton and Oldfield families had known each other for decades and one marrying into the other would have made perfect sense. One family can work the land but two can conquer it.

I don't know much about the rest of Lorrie's life except that she was the victim of physical and emotional abuse over a long period of time. Many were the weekends when she sat outside the Birdsville pub with her seven children waiting for George to finish getting drunk. And when she wasn't being verbally lashed or physically assaulted, the children were. George was, above all else, a bully. He believed his sons should be set against each other like fighting dogs and he often contrived scenarios in which they would inevitably come to blows.

The station had a milking cow and my grandfather would send two of his sons the vast distance to fetch it and bring it in. He would not tell either one he had also sent the other. And one of them he sent on motorbike, the other on foot. Neither dared come home without the cow because, though it seems on the face of it to be a game, George's wrath would consume the loser.

'They were just petrified those boys, absolutely petrified. They lived in terror, they did,' Geoff Morton tells me. 'George would make 'em all sleep outside in that little sleepout. I'd go down there to spend time with them, you know, and two of them would sleep under the bed. And Acre [Rodney] was one of them. And the reason was because they were frightened that during the night their father would come in with a stick and flog them.'

Geoff continues: 'I will always remember as a little fella being out there and George was in the shed and he yelled out, "Jennifer, bring that Jeep over, just drive it across here". Of course it had a crate on the back of it and ... she drove it under this electrical wire and pulled it down with the crate. He never said anything. He just went and got one of those big square screwdriver things and flogged her until she couldn't stand up. I would only have been little and it's been stuck in my brain forever. He flogged her and flogged her and flogged her, and she only did exactly what he told her to do. He was a violent man. She would have been ten or eleven.'

Most of the Morton men are barrels with legs. Their beer bellies surge out and hang below the waists of their jeans. They never learned to walk softly on this great Earth. My father was not any of these things, rather a throwback to his own grandfather. Scrawny and short, he could have been taken by a gentle breeze. His father called him Acre because they ran 1.6 million acres on Pandie Pandie and Rodney was a speck on it, so Acre he was.

'He was always shaking, shaking, but when George was away he was fine. Those boys were different boys,' Geoff says. 'It was psychological terrorism, really. It was both physical and mental abuse.'

From around the age of four, Rodney's brothers would throw him on the back of one of the stallions that had yet to be broken in. He would be terrified by the experience, which would be brought to a stop by the only one who ever really looked out for him, his older brother Craig. Throughout his childhood, Rodney was belittled and bullied and belted across the head for the slightest of transgressions. On one occasion, his father threw a camp oven at him, splitting open his face.

Danielle Weston, who owns the service station in Windorah, the last major stop before approaching Birdsville from the south, has known the Mortons for years. 'They're all fucken queer, fightin' and arguing amongst themselves,' she says to me. 'You're bloody lucky you got out of there, I mean really, because I tell you what, I couldn't have done it.'

In discussing the years of abuse, and conceding that suffered by Lorrie at the hands of her husband, my own mother still projects her instincts on to the woman. 'I will never understand how she could sit there and watch him do that to her children day after day after day,' she says. What could she have done, I ask.

Lorrie, like her children, was trapped. Hemmed in by desert, locked in by 1960s and 70s Australia. Divorce rates over the past 100 years were never lower than they were in the 1960s. The arrival of feminism in the same period failed to unearth domestic violence as a concern. That didn't come until later, helped in part by scenes in London when the first women's refuge opened in Chiswick in 1971, and the publication of a book in 1974 by journalist Erin Pizzey called *Scream Quietly or the Neighbours Will Hear*. Family violence didn't enter the lexicon of Australian federal legislation until 1975 and, even then, a cultural lethargy ensured it stayed hidden for decades more.

Lorrie had nowhere to go. Women's shelters didn't exist then in Queensland or South Australia. There were two in all of Sydney at the time, though they offered no financial assistance and sheltered women and their children only at night. My grandmother had seven children and a husband prone to rage, and lived almost an hour's drive from the nearest civilisation, the town of Birdsville, which today has a population of 300 people. She needn't have screamed quietly. There was no-one else around to hear.

My mother, who would up-end her own life to guard her children against such fury, saw Lorrie's world through her own crises. How Lorrie could do what she did is the question I have asked myself. Not as a matter of judgement but of understanding. How was it that she did not break, not even once? I try to imagine the parameters of her loneliness. She probably wouldn't have called it that.

I doubt, too, that Lorrie had ever heard of the Stoic philosophers with whom she shared much. Nero's counsellor, Seneca, reduced Lorrie's life to a sentence centuries before she was born. In helping to create the very field of Stoicism, Seneca embodied the kind of broad outlook Lorrie employed without ever giving it a name. 'What need is there to weep over parts of life? The whole of it calls for tears,' he wrote.

It seems a simple image, but in those breathless and superheated summer months, Lorrie would spend the hottest part of her day around a wood-fired stove in a stifling kitchen, brewing boiling cups of tea while she made lunch for her husband, kids and the jackaroos. Stoic. The whole of her life may have called for tears, so she rarely produced any. The Stoic mantra, and hers, was simply: *We will survive this*. Lorrie instead turned her attention to working within the confines of her husband's tyranny, and that of the outback itself, to forge the faintest of daily victories. She crept through the gaps of George's attention to do what he would never have allowed otherwise: tell the children they were loved.

The power in the relationship between my grandparents only shifted that one time, when George was faced with charges for assault, and Lorrie seized this sliver of a moment for herself and her children. She was not a passive victim in this life but one who knew clearly the extent of her ability to change the rules. Lorrie knew when she'd been dealt a hand. Her children would be educated if all she did was tell a lie to the justice system—the same system she likely never saw as hers anyway.

Lorrie died of heart problems in 1993 so we cannot ask her how she felt about betraying another woman in an even worse position than she was in, to grant her own kids a chance. Despite the time, Aboriginal people in this particular part of Queensland grew up with the white settler kids and visited each other's homes. Many of them are still friends today and Aboriginal stockmen have become station managers. My own father remembered pieces of the language of local tribes, most notably the words for 'emu run fast'. Still, there was no overcoming race, and Lorrie must have known the power of her decision to help her children at the expense of a black woman.

My father got his two years in boarding school, though none of his siblings stayed in formal education past the age of fifteen. Perhaps it was the bargain, perhaps tight-arse George resented spending station money on his children, but Rodney came home to danger and rage. It was during this time that my father tried to plunge a screwdriver into his own dad's chest and was kicked out of the house. 'Whenever George was home he [Rodney] wasn't allowed in the house,' Geoff Morton tells me.

Rodney could not leave the station. He might have tried walking off but doing so might also have killed him. So he slept rough down by the creek and slinked home late at night. There, after George had passed out, asleep or drunk, Lorrie would leave a plate of food on the verandah for her son. Neither would see the other but she knew he came because the food was always gone.

My grandmother was in occupied territory, working behind enemy lines to do what little she could. 'Your father was treated worse than a dog,' says my mum.

This particular episode went on for weeks, but it's around this time that the chronology breaks down. Maybe these were my dad's final moments on Pandie Pandie, or perhaps things settled down again and he stayed a while longer. The end of his childhood, for want of a better term, came when his eldest sister Jennifer, who'd visited the station from Adelaide, was preparing to return to that city. Dad sat in the passenger seat of her car and said, 'I need you to take me to Adelaide.'

It was half statement, half act of desperation. They were not especially close and she had long been favoured by her father. Jennifer had been conditioned like all the rest: to fear her dad, and when in his graces, to avoid sabotaging it at all costs.

'I can't do that,' she told him.

I've since seen the look of despair my father's face can conjure, even when there are no tears. It all gets channelled into his eyes, the way the waters from Cooper Creek get funnelled into Lake Eyre. I've seen this look in other people, too, though never quite as sharp. It is as if all the memories of horror he has witnessed get pushed forward from some crevice in his brain and into the eyes themselves, which become fat with pain. I know this is the look he gave Jennifer, this beaten and broken teenaged boy trying to outrun his father.

'I'm not getting out of this car,' he told her.

And he didn't, and she drove.

As the twentieth century wore on, the predominance of the bush—a handy catch-all term for any stretch of Australia inland of major regional centres—began to fade as the population centre of the country started to shift. Rural areas suffered a decline in population every year from the turn of the century until 1971, when the trend stabilised. By the time of the 1996 Census, Australia's rural population had fallen 3 per cent from 1947, while the number of metropolitan residents jumped by 125 per cent in the same period and outer-urban areas grew by 176 per cent.

The 2016 Census showed that two-thirds of Australians now live in capital cities and these are growing at twice the rate of regional areas—10.5 per cent compared with 5.7 per cent. New migrants, typically from Asia, are more likely to settle in cities, unlike their European forebears.

A mining boom at the end of the century, tailing off in the 2000s, was a one-off blip in an economy that otherwise concentrated effort and labour in the major cities. The centrifugal forces of that economy, together with higher education reforms, opened up access to universities which themselves had a habit of taking people from regional areas and never giving them back.

The arid back blocks of Australia, often hit by droughts that swallow years, proved fertile grounds for the cultivation of disdain. Its roots were in this demographic massacre of national myths, myths which my family happened to live, and the apparent inability of this new class of Australian to understand what was lost.

It's not that the land was vacated entirely. The properties still existed. But increasingly they were merged or taken under the control of single families or, later, investment vehicles. A way of life, for all its faults, was obliterated and many bowed out. Those who stayed behind amassed great riches. Those who left found fortunes flagging in the bush towns and even in the cities. The decline of the regions continued apace and there was a sense among its long-term residents that something had been taken from them.

A similar sense is fuelling Geoff Morton when he says that his uncle George was 'a total bastard' of a man 'who managed to make things worse from the grave'. My cousin Peter's wife Kylie Morton confirms a story I had heard on the grapevine: George Morton had promised Pandie Pandie Station to my uncle David but he ensured David could never own it. George Morton had a tax bill of $6 million when he died in 2006, representing years' worth of wilful neglect. Pandie Pandie Station was sold two years later for $7.5 million, to pay the debt. After seventy years, it had left the Morton family altogether.

'There was one comment David made before they sold Pandie that absolutely broke my heart, and this is before we were married and with kids,' Kylie says. 'That was David showing emotion. He started to get all worked up about it, quite angry, and he said George had drilled into him that he was never ever to sell Pandie and that he was to hold on to it and pass it down to his son. George treated all his kids like shit, but for David to hold on to that and believe in that and then not be able to do it because of what George had done, it breaks my heart.'

Tragedy is a snake upon the continent, undulating through the thousands of years. The dispossession of Aboriginal people came first, blunt and traumatic, followed by the self-inflicted wounds of families like my own in places already well-versed in suffering.

They were a grain of sand pushed aside by the belly of the serpent; a speck among countless others that gave the earth its raw, red hue.

My father escaped the world into which he was born, physically at least. But the truth of his exit is far more complex. He hasn't stopped running from his father. He can't throw off his past, not even at a sprint.

To understand a person, you must understand his father. This is true of Rodney and it is true of myself, too. Ours is a trauma passed from one generation to another, family heirlooms that are bequeathed by the living. There is an emotional and financial poverty that flows from these wounds.

Crucially, however, our story is also that of a mother who tried to love enough for the failures of everyone around her. This is a foray into an Australia on the outside of public consciousness, one whose egalitarian core is ruptured by ordeals of illness and poverty, and people who have never been taught how to be vulnerable and, in so doing, make misery wherever they go.

Like my father, I made it out, but we have both lost things along the way.

When my grandfather first heard that his own father, CC Morton, had died, he laughed before adding: 'Well, he won't do that again.' Decades later, when George Morton died, one of his sons, David, offered a curt acknowledgement: 'They should just drag his body out into the flat and let the crows pick his eyes out.'

Try as they might to contain the damage, it seeped through, father to son and father to son. Desolation moved like a slinky through them all.

CHAPTER 3

AFTER THE LIGHT

I was six when I watched my brother burn and a lifetime older when the flames were finished with him.

The day it happened, in September 1994, Toby and I were hunting crows with our .22 rifle, which had an ever so slightly crooked barrel. Actually, I hated guns. My cousin had once loaded a rifle with a portion of orange peel and convinced my brother to stand in front of it with his shirt lifted. It was a bad idea, I offered, but my advice was taken in the manner of all advice given by five-year-olds to older boys. There was little victory in being right when my brother doubled over in pain from a fragment of fruit buried in his abdomen.

When life gives you oranges, you should never load them into guns and fire them at your familial line.

The crows hated the guns more than I did. We'd bagged two by the time lunch rolled in, with the outback sun making it unbearable to be outside for long at all.

We had lived on Mount Howitt cattle station for a couple of years by then. This is a place so isolated and treacherous it is most famous for being the region where the explorers Burke and Wills perished after thinking it would be appropriate to take 20 tonnes worth of equipment, including an oak table and apparently zero grams of sense, on the longest continental crossing possible in Australia. We lived in the part of the country that subverted every horror movie convention: white people died first and often.

Mount Howitt was named after the anthropologist Alfred William Howitt, who led the search expedition tasked with finding out what, precisely, had happened to Burke and Wills. And what had happened to them was death and tragedy.

It was a lengthy experiment but Burke and Wills proved ignorance was deadly. A real team effort. My father knew this but he was the son of that hulking, pragmatic man who was himself the son of a man so practical that the middle name given to all of his children, including the girls, was Villiers, after the motor engine. Celsus Charles Morton loved the engine so much he had children, all the better to venerate it.

I'm not sure my father told my mother any of this or else, I'd like to think, she would never have married him—certainly would never have had children with him. A family so besotted with the accoutrements of the industrial revolution is really no family at all. Hadn't they heard how all the children were treated in those factories? They were pulling little corpses out of chimneys for years.

Cattle stations are dangerous places. They were particularly so before the arrival of the Royal Flying Doctor Service. That is to say, before the invention of flight itself. Before then, if you wandered into a nest of brown snakes or your leg fell off or a bull gored the bits of you that aid life, the most pertinent course of medical action was to scream dramatically at the sky, which was very big and very blue and not at all likely to respond. If you were lucky, nature would take its course quickly and you could die proud of the fact you didn't tempt fate quite so invitingly as Burke and Wills.

The Flying Doctor was the brainchild of a Presbyterian minister, John Flynn, who took bush medicine to the outback, establishing little hospitals in far-flung places. The idea only came to fruition, however, in 1928 thanks to a large donation by the manufacturer of the Sunshine Harvester, HV McKay. Later, Flynn's successor as head of the Australian Inland Mission, Reverend Fred McKay (no relation), would come to rebuild the Birdsville Hospital after a devastating fire, thanks to the help of a donation from my great-grandfather, CC Morton. A report in the *Chronicle* newspaper out of Adelaide in 1952 said the pastoralists and many others decided to chip in on account of the story of two nurses who fled the previous year's hospital fire in their nightwear.

'Mona Henry and Lilian Whitehead preferred to stay on,' the report says. 'They lived in a bough shed on which they wrote "Business as Usual" and cooked their meals in a tent. A few weeks later the mailman's wife came in and had an infant.'

Before he passed, Reverend Flynn told harrowing stories about the odds of survival in remote Australia. In summary, they were not very good.

In 1917, a stockman by the name of Jimmy Darcy was hurt in a fall near Halls Creek. It took his mates twelve hours to transport him the 50 kilometres to the town itself, where the postmaster knew some first aid but needed assistance. Attempts to telegraph doctors in nearby communities failed, so the postmaster telegraphed his former first-aid lecturer, a Dr Holland, who was 2000 kilometres away in Perth. Having diagnosed the injuries by Morse code, Dr Holland instructed the postmaster through two bladder surgeries with a pen knife before making the ten-day journey to help by boat, Model T Ford, horse and sulky and, eventually, on foot.

The stockman died the day before the doctor arrived.

Precisely a century later, people in remote and rural Australia still die earlier and faster than their urban peers, and quite avoidably. Research by the Royal Flying Doctor Service, which now caters to an area the size of Western Europe (and in my stretch of the country, wings its way around a dainty chunk the size of the United Kingdom), shows that half of the nation's fatal car accidents happen on rural roads, despite two-thirds of us living in the cities. Agricultural workers die at a rate nine times greater than those in any other industry. Poisoning deaths happen at 3.5 times the rate they do in cities. Physical assaults lead to death at 3.8 times the urban rate, and children in very remote areas, like we were, are 2.2 times more likely to be hospitalised for injury.

In the hidden corners of Australia, the statistics will eventually come for you.

We grew up and lived in an eternal trick perspective box, but instead of the horizon appearing ever reachable it was a rifle or a gun. Once my mum spied a brown snake slithering along an internal wall of a shed and my father grabbed a .303 rifle, apparently from immediately behind him, and fired it into the wall. He killed the snake but the plastering really took a hit.

So I wish I could say that shooting crows that morning was some sort of cosmic omen, but I'd always been haunted by the vague spectre of death. Nothing felt different, everything was in its place.

The corrugated-iron shed at the edge of the homestead was long and usually accommodated a Caterpillar machine used for grading weather-worn roads, several utes, and a mechanics workshop designed to intimidate people like me. In large white letters painted on the roof, the radio frequency: VH-9GN. In this shed, Toby and

I would wear our father's welding helmet and pretend we were a Ned Kelly spaceman, staring with impunity at the sun and the knife of flame spouting from the oxyacetylene torch which sliced through metal with the ease of chemistry.

On this day, one of the jackaroos was fixing a motorcycle when he lost a bolt in the car servicing pit. It's no more fancy than the name suggests: a wooden trapdoor lifts off and the workers can stand underneath a vehicle driven overhead and let out oil and fuel and whatever other black magic powers such industry. This is an old tale. Jackaroo loses bolt in pit, sends boy to collect, boy loses bolt in the dark, asks for a torch. How about a light?

I should have known what would come of the potent combination of naked flame and accelerants. Toby and I were firebugs, genetically pure. In an exercise of extreme folly, we once decided to cleanse the hay shed of mice by setting fire to the tiniest, most controlled corner of it. We'd be hailed as heroes, we thought, as we struck a match. Dad came running just as the smoke started to kick up, giving the mice time to make a break for it as he doused the flames.

It is an unhelpful fact of human nature that a crisis averted is a lesson never learned. We would have set fire to the house, if Dad had let us, and what advice to the contrary could possibly come from a man who had blasted out a wall to kill a snake? Nothing with any gravitas.

So my brother took the lighter and I peered over the edge of the pit, waiting for the light to burrow into the shadow and reveal the puzzle. It happened, as these things so often tend to happen, in the infinitesimal space between seconds. But it takes longer, of course. The smallest moments have a habit of engorging themselves on misery. They swell in size, fill entire universes with dread and worry and fear. In the fabric between space itself these moments expand infinitely, vast membranous fields on which whole civilisations are born and slain. The sum total of human misery, it seemed, played out in this picosecond of horror. My brother, the boy on fire.

Physically, I know the fireball came first but it's his screams I remember the most. The outback is so void of anything substantial it would take an awful lot to fill it up. But his screams filled it up like a boiling kettle, a bubbling agony so fierce I half expected the sky to shatter and the space above to rush in. It was a fireball that engulfed him and turned his flesh to heat. The jackaroo tried to grab him, to fling him out of the pit, but Toby was so hot he had to let go. My father was 300 metres or so away, breaking in horses at the stables.

In my mind there is no middle, just a jump cut to the frantic rush to the homestead. It was Father's Day, and there was Dad, cradling Toby in his arms while skin hung from his son like curtains. The screams had given way to convulsions. I remember this scene but I cannot place myself in it. It's as if I am watching from a security camera. I am disembodied, floating alongside it all like a spirit.

My father is racing now, a hidden man fading away even as he carries the burning boy. He is racing so far ahead of himself, breaking forth from this exoskeleton, all soft in the light. Exposed.

Hundreds of kilometres away, the Royal Flying Doctor Service crew was returning to Charleville after their biggest day of the year— keeping a medical eye on the thrumming crowds at the Birdsville Races, where the horses race on dirt and the pub has been known to run out of beer. In the course of our short time on the station, the crew had come to know us by name. Specifically Toby, for he was an enthusiastic student of misfortune.

Once, my brother demonstrated a remarkable ability to scale the pole supporting the stairs leading up to the second floor of the house, a routine that suffered from an over-efficient dismount and the cracking of his head on the floor. It was one of the more remarkable moments of suturing the Flying Doctor crew had performed because they were met on the dusty airstrip by my mother carrying my brother followed by myself, the blue heeler, the pet lamb—an idiot—and the cat. The car had a flat battery and Dad was away. There was no explanation for the menagerie except that they were probably as bored as my brother was before his ascent and had been led to the airstrip under false pretences. It was no Noah's Ark and salvation was not coming for them or, indeed, any of us. They stitched up my brother under the wing of the plane and sent us, dog and cat and idiot sheep included, on our way.

On another occasion, Toby was mucking about on the trampoline with our governess when he was caught in the at-once exhilarating and terrifying physics of a double-bounce, the alignment of the mat and the other participant just so that it propels you at speed into the ether. What goes up must come down, and what gets double-bounced must be catapulted into the concrete footpath at force, such is the way of these things. It was concussion, the doctors ruled over the wireless radio. Toby spent the night in Charleville hospital.

One of the great marvels of the Flying Doctor is its invention of the standardised medical chest, a jungle-green metal box filled with numbered medicines, pain relief and bandages, some of which are prescription only. Trampled by beasts? Take a 24. Arm caught in a fencing rig? Dose yourself up on the pain relief and wait for the evac flight. There is a number for almost all that ails you, short of broken hearts and conditions that bring a near immediate onset of death.

Toby. The neighbours were coming from forty minutes away to provide steady hands to unsteady parents. My brother was flailing or perhaps shivering on the floor of the schoolroom where the wireless radio was located. We used to do long-distance learning over two-way radio with a teacher based in a bush town 370 kilometres to the east. I loved shouting my name into the handset whenever I had the answer to a question. But now my parents were shouting into it for help, for the plane. A voice delivered in the crackle of static dispassionately administered medical instructions. There were numbers, the medical chest was unlatched, and my brother shivered.

I remember thinking: Why is he shivering? Is he cold? I could see that his face had swelled to what seemed twice its normal size. The severe burns had produced a thick and gruesome build-up of fluids beneath his skin that had, essentially, been cauterised.

It was marching towards the end of daylight when we called for the plane, which was a problem. The Flying Doctor has rules, and the first among them is their planes will not land or take off in the dark. The pilots need to see the runway and it wouldn't be the first time if they struck a kangaroo. Besides, bush airstrips are small affairs, glorified hectares of compacted dirt with little cones along the edges under which some birds nest. My brother and I would lift these cones up to grab the chicks, occasionally finding rare marsupials or entire snakes coiled like springs. Without fail they were always angry at the intrusion and, without fail, we'd put the cone back down and go on looking elsewhere.

On this airstrip I learned to ride my first motorbike, the PeeWee 50, and on this airstrip my brother, doubled pillion on the back, told me to slow down for the first time ever. It was smooth, like riding on gossamer. Where planes took gently to flight at the end of it, however, a harsh and gravelled mess awaited the bike rider if his addiction to speed outlasted his internal conflict about hitting the brakes.

A second truth of the Flying Doctor, which nobody mentioned, was that my brother would die if the plane was stranded. Fortunately, beetroot tins were on hand.

Going to town usually meant a three-hour trip to Quilpie and was a rare enough event that we'd become excited by the simple things, like the sound of traffic and the concept of shops. I'd become rich at an early age, finding myself in possession of nine one-dollar coins, which back then could purchase, I reasoned, my first investor property or at the very least ten of the prettiest horses in the west. My father didn't like that I quality-controlled my horses in terms of how pretty they were but it was a metric that mattered to me, and I was rich enough now to enforce it. Instead, I bought nine Cherry Ripes at the pub and ate half of them so quickly I vomited, earning the wrath of my father and losing the title of 'pretty horse mogul' which, in retrospect, was a blessing.

If outback stations are a harsh environment for most in Australia, towns were a strange amalgam of behaviours to the rest of us. We never chose to stay long, so these trips were usually for one thing: buying carloads of non-perishables like tinned corn, powdered milk and other necessities such as beer and Log Cabin tobacco for Dad. But it was the beetroot that, as it turned out, saved my brother.

The super-sized empty cans were filled with kerosene and set on fire. I drove up with Dad to the airstrip as the sun set and we laid the cans along its edges, rudimentary guiding lights for the plane, which had landed after refuelling in Charleville. Fire had tried to kill my brother but it would orient his rescuers, too.

The crew put a drip in Toby on the runway in case turbulence made it impossible to do on the flight, and he was loaded into the belly of the plane, a wounded sardine being slipped back into the can. My mother climbed aboard with Lauryn, just three weeks old. My father attempted to stop her; he wanted her to stay with him. His own loneliness frightened him more than the loneliness of his son. This suffusive loneliness was what would, ultimately, destroy our family.

Mum knew how much my father hurt from the time when, as a five-year-old, he was shipped off to emergency in Adelaide alone.

There was no way my mother was leaving her own son in similar circumstances. She was painfully aware of the ideas that would germinate within him if he were to survive. A medley of instances can make children grow wrong. She knew this because she loved a man who had grown crooked.

I went to get on board too, but Mum stopped me at the stairs. There was no room. Be strong back here, she said. My father needed me. The boy who would collect the pretty horses, ultimate comforter of a hard and ruined man.

The pilots radioed ahead to Charleville where they would need to refuel again to make the trip to Brisbane. They ordered pizza to meet them at the base—it had been hours since anyone had eaten and they would need the sustenance. A doctor on the flight, Bob, would later tell a family friend that my mother was the strongest woman he had ever met. Calm, a granite composure. She straddled her two new worlds with the kind of grace that only reveals itself in a furnace: a newborn's mother and the mother of a critically injured child. Her love underwent a cellular division and it existed simultaneously for my sister and brother in the crisp air. The plane rocked in the curious silence of the emergency and she rocked with it.

Burned at 2 p.m., in Brisbane by 10 p.m. But no ambulance met them at the airport, despite the calls from the crew. Doctor Bob was furious and refused the handover when the ambulance finally arrived half an hour later, instead travelling with my family to the hospital. It would be midnight before my brother made it into the burns unit. I did not know any of this.

I recall the plane disappearing into the ink of the night, its propeller engines buzzing like emergency vital signs in the sky. And then I recall nothing at all. Nothing for weeks. It's as if somebody rushed into the projector room and cut the film. The drama over,

I remember nothing of its natural diminuendo. It is a shame because such little detail may have been revealing to how we—my father and I—ultimately dealt with the shock. Did he drink? He usually drank, so perhaps this night he did not. Did he spend his time with me and I with him? What did I do? It feels as if my mind betrayed my body, allowed it to wander off unaccounted for.

Trauma, we now know, has a knack for worming its way into your bones. My body was sentenced to this fate in those dark, blank weeks and my mind was sentenced in absentia. Such stress casts a long, rank shadow over the life of a child. It imprints itself on some 3000 sites in your DNA and on every chromosome and it grows with you, like a knotted tree around a stake.

The lives of my brother and I can be measured in distinct plots: the short, hyper-realistic years before the fire and the dark decades since in which the initial event metastasised into something deadly, a poison coursing through our veins. The fire destroyed our foundation, and the accumulating moments on top of it have threatened to topple ever since. Before the fire our childhood was an idyllic sandpit, played out on 2500 square kilometres of rock and dirt. If there was a nagging sensation it would all come to nought, we did not feel it.

I was an anxious child but my brother drummed it out of me with his insistence on doing dangerous things, like jumping gullies on the motorbike or chasing wild pigs with tusks the size of our hands. He cut my anxiety to ribbons and diluted it with the cavernous blue sky of the west. It wriggled, occasionally, but a wriggle in an ocean is a speck.

It did not wriggle on that Father's Day. It ought to have. You've seen the end of the horror movie when you cast back. You've seen the major players marching inexorably to their fate and you want to scream at them. Don't go into the shed! Don't take the lighter! But they go into the shed and they take the lighter and you peer over the edge of your mind like you peered over the edge of that oil-slicked pit.

There are flames.

CHAPTER 4

ALIEN LIFE

I didn't speak English for the first few years of my life. It wasn't any other native tongue, either. My father couldn't understand me. For all her efforts, Mum struggled. Their boy lived in something of a language bubble that made each of them wonder what they had managed to produce.

Toby, a few years older, was the only one capable of comprehending my youthful gurgles, mangled words and dial-up-modem sounds. He was not exactly a linguistic genius. The broadest range of his vocabulary—a set of sweeping profanity—presented itself just once when he stole a baby emu out from under the nose of its incredibly fast father. He understood me, however.

Toby was enlisted as my interpreter in this world with which I could not connect. It was a fairly limiting job because I hated talking to people and tried to avoid them as best I could, which was mostly very easy in our isolation. Occasionally, Mum would wander into the lounge room and find me parked in front of the television watching a French-language news service, apparently engrossed.

Other days, Spanish. Some days, neither of us knew what country's bulletin I was tracking, though the men all had moustaches and there was lots of smoke.

The station had a cook called Melissa, whom I called Issa. My name was Ricky but I couldn't say it properly, introducing myself as Icky. I'd have made a bad pirate. A stranger would respond, 'Oh, your name is Icky?', and I would scream at them: 'No, it's Icky!' And we would continue on in this fashion until one of us died.

The incomprehensible gibber came to a sudden end one day when my father sat on my hand and wouldn't respond to my pleas for help. They didn't make sense, as usual, because I was half farmyard animal and half boy. Mum tells the rest of the story: 'Then you just looked up at your father and said, clear as day, "You don't understand me do you?".'

It was as if I couldn't trust my own family with clarity until that moment. I was about two or three but had never seen a doctor about my speech. Mum never had a single scan while she was pregnant with me; we just lived too far away from the hospital.

The incident served as confirmation for my father that I was not his son and proof to my mother that I was also not hers, at least not according to the strict definitions usually applied to motherhood. She had long suspected it, chasing my father around the house and yelling at him: 'He's different, Rodney. Can't you see that?' To her, it was inexplicable. Two parents, neither of whom had finished high school, produced a boy who liked mustering cattle and being outdoors. This makes sense to anyone who learned about Punnett squares in Year 8 biology. Then I came along with my bird-like limbs, wide eyes and hesitant approach to the world.

I studied everything from a distance before becoming involved, if I became involved at all. Loud noises annoyed me and minute fluctuations in my routine—such as leaving the house, or breakfast—

upset me. I couldn't speak properly, was almost certainly going to be gay, and one day showed Mum I could read by completing all the answers in my school workbook while her back was turned.

In an ordinary environment, such as a city family, these milestones would be seen as a credit to the parents and their tutelage of their son, probably called Rupert or Harrison if we are being honest. Their son would be the result of their efforts in the same way a pavlova is the product of oppressive forces like whisking. Every child born in the city is 1500 mandatory violin lessons away from greatness.

Mum saw no such reason to claim responsibility and when I was at an early age she first explained to me my providence, in earnest tones. 'You're not my son,' she said. 'The aliens left you under the cabbage patch to observe humanity and one day you'll have to go back and tell them what you saw.'

The news ought to have shocked me but it did not. In the normal fashion, children who are told they are adopted—be it from Africa or interstellar supreme floating intelligences—tend to have a bad reaction. Maybe they try to run away, maybe they rebel and take up the flute. To me, however, it made sense. Of course these people were not my parents. They liked horseriding and checking the rain gauge. They did things that confused me. Dad played polocrosse in outback events, a game that seemed to have been invented by someone who liked neither fun nor meaning, possibly an economist.

Our nearest neighbours were half an hour away by car, the nearest town an hour or more. We only had each other, in that sense, but even so my family never felt like they were mine. I watched them as if through glass at the zoo: observing, wondering how they came to me, analysing what would happen if the glass fell in and they rushed from the enclosure. Other days, I was the one enclosed—the boy in the bubble.

Our mythology did not burn away with the years. During the dark times to come, Mum would ruffle my hair and whisper: 'You're certainly going to have a lot to tell the aliens.' Neither of us had read Nora Ephron, but this phrase became our variant of 'Everything is copy'. Even the worst experiences became fodder for my eventual report back.

The stories continued into high school, when Mum would watch TV news reports of strange phenomena around the world. Unexplained lights in the sky, weird weather patterns. Crop circles. 'That's the aliens looking for you,' she would say from her armchair without a hint of a joke. In our very small world, the many permutations of this phrase became our own cultural touchstone. The longest narrative arc in my existence, the piece of thread to which my mother and I clung. Proof that despite it all, we had not been replaced by mutant beings. We were us, still.

There were times when our reliance on the alien MacGuffin perplexed even me and I called Mum out on it. 'Sometimes you seem so serious I feel like I actually am adopted or you know something I don't and you're using the aliens thing as a cover story,' I prodded her on more than one occasion. These little interludes would end in hysterics, Mum in tears, laughing, and me in pretend outrage: 'Just admit it, you stole me from an orphanage run by dogs!'

Not once has she broken the fourth wall and admitted it was just a story of domestic exceptionalism, a way to frame her belief that I was special. Every parent thinks they have a special child. Some of them actually do, though why would anyone believe them in the chorus? You know these parents. Mr 8 was beating Russians in chess by the time he could walk. Miss 11 was a founding member of The Saddle Club. Thomas invented double-entry bookkeeping for the Venetians. The difference for us was that Mum couldn't bring herself to take the credit.

When I became a cadet journalist in 2005, it was meant to be, Mum said, because this was how the aliens could make sure I gathered enough information. Sure, outwardly I was working for a large regional daily newspaper, but inwardly I was an intergalactic researcher, sent from the heavens to sniff out the essence of humanity and pop it in a dossier. At times, though, I desperately hoped the fantasy could be true. At night, when I heard Mum crying in the room opposite because Dad had stopped paying child support again, I tried to imagine that all of this, all of our suffering, had been for something.

Maybe it was just for a story, the right to tell someone else about us. I imagined being beamed up into some orbiting alien spacecraft and urged to brief them on what I had found so far. And I could tell them the story of humanity from the beginning, if the moment struck me. I would tell them that the oldest written story we have is the 'The Epic of Gilgamesh' and that it contains the not insignificant detail of a man, created by a god, who sustains an erection for seven days and seven nights.

We told stories before that, too. Ones that were never written down. Had I known it at the time—had the world known it—I might have also explained that the Neanderthals who preceded and briefly overlapped with us Homo sapiens made jewellery and buried their dead. That they plucked the dark feathers from birds, possibly for ceremonial use. Never the white feathers.

They did these things, I would elaborate, because they had found a reason to do so. Because they told each other stories. Neanderthals likely had high-pitched, gravelly voices. If you were to go back in time to visit, it is quite likely that our ancestor's story time would sound like a small animal being run over on an unsealed road.

Henry Molaison, I'd venture, had an operation in 1953 to treat epilepsy but which ended up destroying his hippocampus and amygdala. This wiped out the story of Henry's life, the picture reel we all have that tells us who we are and from where we have come. Henry lived for many years but he never formed new memories for more than thirty seconds. Every half-minute his world would reset and he would forget, again, that his parents were dead. When he was told they had died, he grieved once more. And then they slipped away, lost to him all over again.

But in my own mind that is not the report I handed back to the aliens in space, the ones who had sent for me. The only story I wanted to tell them, in those lonely moments when I imagined being summoned instead of trying to sleep, was that Mum was the hero. I wanted them to know, even if she didn't, that she had prevailed.

There are shades of victory, I know. Winning, in our sense, meant subsisting. Nothing more. In a way, our family became a version of Henry Molaison. After we were cleaved from our old life and thrust into the new one, there could be no more living, just surviving. Our most interesting memories all existed from a time before this violent fracture and we repeated them, as if to solidify them in our minds.

When I moved out of home to start work, my phone calls with Mum would often revert to discussions of my father's dysfunctional family: the brutality of my paternal grandfather, the court case to win control of Barraroo Station from him, my father's own emotional and physical attacks on Mum. When she was angry, she told my brother, sister and I that we had inherited his bad qualities. Or in lighter moments she'd say to my sister: 'Geez you walk like your father, Loz.'

We heard all the same stories on a loop. None of us could have known that by plucking these memories out and rolling them around the contours of our tongue, enunciating them, we were also destroying them, making them less real.

Plato saw memories as fallible, approximations only of what was truly real. They were impressions left on a wax tablet and easily erased. Writing in the 'Timaeus', Plato likened our memories to portraits or landscapes painted on the canvas of the soul by an internal artist. Up until recently, most everyone disagreed with Plato, believing memories were formed and immediately stored somewhere in the architecture of the brain. It was 'consolidation', as they called it, and memories were filed like sensitive documents in an archive, perhaps to be collected again or just as likely forgotten in the dust. But around the turn of the second millennium, Karim Nader, a postdoctoral researcher at New York University, demonstrated that one of the biggest memory heresies was, in fact, true.

Nader showed memory was not a thing made once but again and again. He proved the intuition of many in the arts, such as the playwright Eugène Ionesco, who once wrote: 'I am not quite sure whether I am dreaming or remembering, whether I have lived my life or dreamed it. Just as dreams do, memory makes me profoundly aware of the unreality, the evanescence of the world, a fleeting image in the moving water.'

Nader trained rats to fear a sound. In his lab at NYU, he played a tone and then delivered an electric shock to the feet of the animals. He did it many times so that the rats' blood pressure rose when they heard the noise; their fur stood on end. The world knew, and so did Nader, that the creation of a memory required some kind of chemical reaction in the brain. But he introduced his own sacrilegious twist: Why was everyone so sure a memory was only created once?

He left his rats alone for a day, to give their newfound fear of the tone time to settle, and then he came back and played it again. This time, however, he injected a drug into the rat's amygdala that prevented the formation of proteins needed to forge memories.

If a memory was formed only once, the drug would not work. But if, by the very act of recalling the memory, the neurons *re-created* it with new proteins, it might disrupt that process.

Nader injected the rats within hours of making them recall the memory—by playing the tone again—and waited. Two weeks later they showed no fear at all. It was as if the memory of the shocks had never happened. Less fortunate rats who received neither drug nor a placebo injection continued on in a state of sound-related anxiety. The good news, one supposes, is that rats tend not to live very long.

Nader's results shattered the status quo: the very act of remembering something could also change it. Memories were not stored in the filing cabinet of the brain. They were reconstructed with proteins each and every time a person needed them. The most pure memory is the one we never come back to. Everything else changes, the wax tablet.

Between us, Mum and I, we wore our memories down. For the aliens, for the story, for some poorly defined purpose neither of us could quite articulate.

The first thing I think I remember, at age two, is a litter of puppies underneath some outdoor stairs on Currawilla Station. Then nothing until moving day at Palparara Station. It is nothing grand, just a faint vignette of me sitting on the linoleum floor playing with a single, yellow Duplo block that had been left out of the packing for me. I remember seeing the bright-blue budgie cage my father had welded for my mother underneath a tree in the dust outside. Perhaps deliberately, it was made from so much metal it was too heavy to move. There was something of a motorcade on our way to the new homestead at Mount Howitt. Several cars, men on motorbikes and five white gates. I remember using one of the three new toilets at Mount Howitt and discovering a rat in it. I didn't shit for days.

When my life outside of home started as a teenager on the Gold Coast, working in my dream career, I began collecting new stories. But amassing more wild stories—bizarre run-ins with powerful figures and the odd outlaw motorcycle gang member—only served to remind me that Mum's story had stopped. Whatever new things I might have to tell her, we would end up back in the past, raking over the coals of our existence. And I stayed there with her, promising myself that if we made it through I would help Mum continue her story.

There are a handful of people in the world with a hyper-accurate memory. Not the ones who can recite pi to 22 000 decimal places. They call what they have a highly superior autobiographical memory, because 'good at remembering stuff' was apparently taken. Two Americans with hyper-accurate memories have revealed what it has done to them.

When Bob Petrella is stuck in traffic, he flicks back through his life and catalogues the best Saturday in every June since he was a child. He remembers every detail of the best days of his life. One of them was when he was sitting on a rooftop age sixteen, listening to a neighbourhood battle of the bands. Jill Price remembers everything that has happened to her on every day of her life since 1980, including on which day each event took place. She remembers the worst days.

Both say their ability developed after learning at a young age that nothing ever stays the same. It's as if they are obsessed with what could have been, hoarding every scrap of information in case it is the best scrap. Jill calls it a 'burden'. She remembers her husband's eyes the day he died. Hearing a date can trigger recall, whether she wants it to or not.

When my brother was taken away to hospital with burns, my own mind went blank. But there are things from the weeks that followed that I have never been able to forget.

I remember, for instance, my father's semen on his bedsheets as they were being taken from his room to be washed by our nineteen-year-old governess. The woman with whom he had been sleeping. The woman who was not my mother. I passed her in the upstairs hallway as she was leaving Dad's room and asked her what the droplet stains were. Water, she'd said.

A seven-year-old is not meant to know what semen looks like, and I didn't, but would later make sense of it all in my head. The memory stayed with me because I knew even then something was happening. They were hiding something.

The first clue came when I attempted an ill-fated game of surprise. Freshly showered, I crept down the stairs of the home-stead at Mount Howitt and snuck up to the doorway that led into the living room. I sprung from around the corner and scared the governess, my father and myself. She was sitting on his lap in the leather recliner, curled in close to his chest. I had never seen my father with another woman before and the circuitry in my head froze. She heard me first and was shot into the air by the force of her own surprise.

I didn't think about this in the moment but it has since occurred to me that my governess was not particularly bright. Nor, for that matter, was my father. Both of these things did not bode well for my education though it gives me some sense of reprieve that my younger self outsmarted them both.

We didn't have much luck with governesses. The first ended up in court after whacking Toby with an iron bar. The second one lasted less than a week, which was just as well because she had such a high-pitched sneeze that dogs would come running whenever she let one off. My mother was a governess when she met my father on Durham Downs Station, an almost 9000-square-kilometre expanse of cattle country in far south-west Queensland. So I guess that's a win, on account of the fact I was born. But governesses three through four were bad news. Especially Vanessa. We called her Vanessa the Undresser even before the affair because slut-shaming hadn't been invented yet. It was the early 1990s and even if we were inclined to be 'woke', in the modern sense, back then it was simply a word that described the condition of waking in the middle of the night to a brown snake in the house.

History now tells me I ought not to have been surprised. A governess worked her way into the English royal family after being employed by John of Gaunt and his children, mothering her own children with him and becoming, eventually, the great-great-grandmother of King Henry VII of England. Louis XIV of France took as his last mistress Madame de Maintenon, the governess of his illegitimate children. And who can forget Maria von Trapp? In fairness to her morals, at least she pounced four years after Agatha von Trapp succumbed to scarlet fever. In Charlotte Brontë's *Jane Eyre*, the governess marries her employer, too. In *Vanity Fair* the governess makes a play at deception in all its many forms to carry her through Regency high society.

The Victorian era was the heyday of the European governess. They were better than servants but not of the same social milieu of their employers. They—young, childless and unwed women all—were expected to live a life of virtual solitude lest they get too close to the master of the house. Good advice, really. The outback Australian version, however, is not the same breed. As near as I can tell, the only requirement of the job is that they be alive. Most of them come from the city, eager for a taste of the bush romanticised by Henry Lawson and Banjo Paterson. Many of them leave quickly, having been acquainted with the version of the bush in which everything they hold dear is trampled, bludgeoned or otherwise beaten to death.

Vanessa was neither from the city nor from one of the grazing aristocracies that peppered the bush. Her family ran a trucking company from Toowoomba and Tambo in Queensland. It appeared not to be the future she wanted for herself, so she raided someone else's instead.

If the lap incident hadn't been the smoking gun, the night I caught Vanessa and my father kissing in the kitchen after dinner was. I went to return my dessert plate and she had one leg wrapped around his and they were going at it. They looked like two shit slinkies that had become stuck together in a drawer. I left quietly and put my plate back on the table. They never saw me.

It is hard to describe the feeling you get as a very small boy, when your mum is 1500 kilometres away with your newborn sister and new-burned brother in a hospital in Brisbane, and you realise you contain a world-shattering secret. Is this how a new president feels when they are handed the nuclear codes after taking the oath?

People with highly superior autobiographical memory have brains with larger regions where memories are created and retained. This is evidence of some correlation, to be sure, but nobody can be certain whether the large brains have come about because the subjects are so good at memory recall, or whether they are so good at memory recall because their brains were abnormally large in the first place. It's a chicken-or-the-egg argument, only in this instance the egg can remember being squeezed out of an asshole. A new theory of memory is emerging, however. And it involves both the mind and the body.

Early stress changes the way genes express themselves. Even if your mind forgets, like mine did in the days after my brother was burned, the body finds a way of remembering. An octopus has entire neural systems—each like mini-brains—in its limbs so they can be moved independently of each other in response to different stimuli. Sometimes, our bodies do the thinking for us, too.

Late one night I made sure I cried loud enough in my room so my father would come in. He asked me what was wrong and, without mentioning the puzzle pieces I had heaved into place, I told him: 'You don't love Mum anymore, do you?' The lie he gave me in return was effortless. It's not that he had practised it—I'm not sure he foresaw his son asking in such a direct manner—but it was easy for him to do because he was the only player in his game. He was fighting for his comfort, not mine. It was a coward's war.

Toby was covered head to toe in brown pressurised bandages when I finally saw him. It took Dad a week to visit. We drove the fourteen hours from the station in silence, save for the tape of Frankie Valli and the Four Seasons in the LandCruiser. Big girls don't cry. My brother had endured round after round of skin grafts. They took whole rectangles of skin from his inner thigh and transferred them to his arms and face. His body looked like farmland from the air, a patchwork of shades and hues and grafts and scorched bits. I remember the way he screamed during shower time at the hospital. His skin stuck to the bandages when they were peeled off and replaced with new ones. Every day was a series of new traumas.

When Dad arrived, he propositioned my mother for sex. When she declined, citing the case of her firstborn lying horrifically injured in the hospital bed, he accused her of having an affair with the doctors while he stayed behind on the station. Dad, abandoned so many times in his own childhood, was convinced of his obsolescence. He saw ghosts leaving him at every turn. In the end, for once, he left first.

Over six weeks passed before Mum returned to Charleville with my brother and sister, now a few months old. Apart from Dad and his mistress, I was the only person who knew about the affair.

Mum, having shepherded the family through one catastrophe, was about to be confronted with a bigger one.

The act of living through post-traumatic stress disorder, they say, is not simply remembering the bad memory but *reliving* the bad experience, as if it were happening all over again. I still feel exactly what it was like to know ahead of time what Mum was walking into and not be able to tell her. Physically, emotionally, lexicographically: I couldn't marshal the resources to do it. I didn't even know the word 'affair' existed.

There is guilt. All you do is think and think and think about the secret you have and it stains you from the inside. Your stomach hurts all day long. My brother and I used to practise holding our breath underwater, going as deep as we could for as long as we could. It felt like those final seconds, before you've made the call to come up for air. Cells screaming, the sense of urgency like tar in the lungs.

Two years before the gun buyback and new laws governing how farmers should store their rifles, we had several guns hanging on a rack in the office on the homestead. The ammo was in a drawer in the same room. 'I was going to shoot them both,' Mum tells me later. 'But I was visited by a guardian angel. I'm not kidding, Rick. A little voice told me to think about you kids. That would have been the end for all of us.'

Voices, angels, divine intervention. There is a favoured saying among believers, for we were counted as believers, and it goes like so: God never gives you more than you can handle. God dispenses Her tests in the same way the progressive tax system collects its revenue. Mum, it turned out, was targeted generously in the first instance.

After telling Mum about the affair, Dad played it safe. He hid Vanessa a half-hour's drive from the homestead, at a dam we had dubbed the Turkey's Nest because it was lined with blue tarpaulin and looked like a giant, circular swimming pool.

Again, my memory ran away. A black hole formed where these events took place, which only closed when we were living in a housing commission in Charleville. There was no money, little hope and four of us. Just like that, our lives had been completely rewritten. The street was in a dysfunctional part of town and Mum's anxiety crackled in the new environment. The neighbours screamed at each other during prolonged domestic disputes deep into the evening. Mum changed Toby's pressure bandages every day—he wore one on his face, arms and legs—and my sister's nappy as needed. Then we all got chickenpox, because life is funny like that.

The alien backstory that started as a whimsical meme between Mum and me now became necessary to give purpose to the pain. This wicked hurt, all of it, was material for the beings who had sent me. So I took notes, committed them to memory. I would have to tell it all some day.

More than two decades later I pop home from Sydney for a visit. Mum beams at me from the garden, where she's ferreting about, pulling up weeds. 'You're home to see your Earth mother,' she says. 'You'll go back someday. They're expecting a report.'

'When do you think they'll come for me?' I say.

'When you've got enough information.'

CHAPTER 5

ZERO-SUM GAME

In the summer of 2017, Mum called me and began sobbing so forcefully I could almost feel the vibrations of her despair through the phone. The school where she had worked for almost two decades as a teacher's aid was losing children and her hours were due to be cut from twenty-eight to twenty-four a week. The difference, as it happened, was that between simply surviving as another member of the working poor and giving in to poverty altogether. 'I thought I'd be further ahead in my life than this, Rick,' she said through tears. 'I'm fifty-seven this year. I don't have any skills. I'm stupid.'

When I was younger and Mum made self-deprecating jokes about not having a degree, I would joyfully remind her that she had a Master's in Life. There was no doubt she felt trapped by her own circumstances, many single parents are, but it was only through her survival instincts that any of her children had grown up at all.

'Mum, you had to run so much harder than anybody else,' I said to her on that call. 'When they were getting degrees and trying other jobs, you were running to keep still. When they made connections and networks, you were raising and loving three kids outside of work.'

We never find the words we want in the eye of the moment. What I desperately wanted her to know was something I'd studied firsthand as I'd grown older. Her station in life wasn't a character flaw, nor her immobility due to lack of effort. She had worked *harder* than anyone else I knew, every day. She had no partner to share the burden in the harder weeks, no money for the hired help, no emotional support. She had always worn that chain adults wear so heavily when they keep secrets the children must never know.

In the year we had this conversation, I paid more in tax than Mum had ever earned *in any year* she raised the three children with which she had been left. It is hard to define the parameters of my own guilt over the situation, for I was constantly broke at the end of each pay cycle, lived more than comfortably, and had had not a single cent of savings through my entire adult life. This continues to be true.

In my close friendship circle, my curiously disastrous financial affairs are the subject of jokes. I am a garbage bin fire of poor life choices powered by a beating heart. Guilty as charged. I feel anger, too. Not at Mum or my upbringing but at a system that equates hard work with success and views families like my own as inherently flawed. After all, if you just work hard everyone gets a shot at the middle class, right? Those left behind in a land of opportunity must be deficient or lazy or plain uninterested. But social mobility is not a train you get to board after you've scraped together enough for the ticket. You have to build the whole bloody engine. Some have nothing to work with except a spoon and hand-me-down psychological distress.

There is a lie we are told in Australian politics and it is usually spread with a sample size of one. The stories of those who made it out are not so rare as to be harmless. You know the type: big grin, slick job, car covered in bumper stickers about hard work. This isn't really true, just a story we fashion for ourselves after the fact. Hard work, though always necessary by the nature of our disadvantage, is not the defining trait that will lift us up from the bottom. Hard work is our version of a dragon eating the sun each day, a tale in place of a reality that remains inexplicable. Climbing free of a past that has entangled you requires a strong work ethic and the right quantity of caprice, in a universe so fluid and changing that to fall into the sweet embrace of such luck is, by definition, insane.

In 1890, based on a then counterintuitive visit to the slums and tenements of New York City, Jacob A Riis produced *How the Other Half Lives*, a remarkably compassionate—for the time—look at a class in society written off by all the others as hopeless drunks and amoral cretins. Across the century-plus since it was written, it has held two of the most clear-eyed sentences I have ever read on the sheer effort it takes to be poor: 'There is nothing in the prospect of a sharp, unceasing battle for the bare necessaries of life, to encourage looking ahead, everything to discourage the effort. Improvidence and wastefulness are natural results.'

Still, Mum blessed us with a strange amount of forward-looking hope when we were young. From my vantage point in the future, it seems to be as alien as a mother who has only ever lived underground trying to explain the stars to her children. What must hope have looked like for her in those first years after the divorce?

Mum worked briefly at a David Jones department store when she left school, travelled for a couple of months in Japan, and then went far north into Queensland's Gulf Country and inconceivably far west, working as a governess on remote properties. Nothing she had done in life before she married our father in her early twenties and had her first child at twenty-four could have prepared her for the stabbing solitude of being a single mum to three children, cast off from the only life she'd ever planned and then thrown back on to the working market a decade after she'd left it.

It was nearing the end of 1994 and Mum's marriage was over, just months after one of her sons was almost killed in a fire. The family bank accounts were frozen, she had no job, and a 1300-kilometre trip to move back near her own family loomed. While she scrimped together cash from government support and booked us on a family sleeper carriage to Ipswich, our father drove the same route with his new squeeze to sign the divorce papers. He didn't offer a cent for his children then or, broadly speaking, ever. In a way those two trips, his in the 4WD and ours crammed into bunks on a slow-moving train, would become symbols of the lives each camp had before them. One, railroaded, the other of his own making. That 4WD, to which both my parents' names were attached, was sold out from underneath my mother. The car dealer never asked for her signature.

At first, I thought Mum was meticulous by dent of her own personality. She had stacks of ruled notebooks in her cupboard in which she noted her expenses and bills, expanding files filled with receipts—and a penchant for rifling through them on her bed at the weekend. There are things all children remember about their childhood homes: the smells, the animals, the way certain pictures hang crooked for years on the tongue-and-groove walls. From the moment we started our new lives, Mum's notebook on the coffee table, filled with sums and numbers, was a constant. It was the perfect kilogram stored in a vault by which we could measure everything else.

Each night, when she wasn't perched with vigilance over her latest cross-stitch pattern, Mum would scribble down her sums. They weren't physics equations but they governed how we might behave in our world nonetheless: how much money she had left in the bank, what bills she had coming up, when she could pay what to avoid both the late fees and running out of food. To a child they looked like large sums of money, though Mum knew they were impossibly small. Within the parameters of these addition and subtraction formulas she had to fit the full breadth of our lives—a son with third-degree burns; a baby daughter; and me, somewhere in the middle, far older than I should have been. She knew how much money she had on any day down to the last five cents because anything less precise was an invitation to financial freefall.

The cruel twist of poverty is that a person with no money pays more for everything. A 2015 Harvard University study by Xavier Jaravel found that those on incomes of less than US$30 000 paid a 2 per cent premium on everyday goods and services. I never needed research to tell me that. It was written in the way we shopped. Mum hunted specials, of course, but when money was tight you could never buy in bulk, nor take advantage of early payment rewards. Interest rates tend to be higher, especially for emergency loans, and one late bill can become a financial echo that lasts for years. When I struggled through my university years, this became doubly apparent, because I never had the mandatory devotion to budgets that Mum did. In a sense, that hangover is still with me all these years later, curled up around my DNA.

That's the essence of where we're at in the way we understand poverty. Epigenetics is an emerging field, one still prone, scientists warn, to the follies of youth and excitement among its researchers. But the evidence is forming a neat package that points to one major finding: poor children have poor bodies.

Take your genes, the precise almanacs that decode your body and who you are. They are rulebooks set out in a double-helix that are copied from generation to generation. This code doesn't change, save for copying flaws in reproduction, but epigenetic markers can attach to the strands of DNA and, in doing so, switch individual genes on or off. In essence, these markers can tell the genes how to behave without ever messing with the fundamental gene. It's nature versus nurture in a very modern sense, and what we have learned is that nurture in the broadest sense matters more than we ever thought possible.

One of the most astonishing examples of this comes from a study in 2014 of the Överkalix people of northern Sweden who were kind enough to make incredibly detailed records of births, deaths, family lines and stores of food stretching back centuries. The cycles of feast and famine allowed researchers Marcus Pembrey, Richard Saffery and Lars Olov Bigren to track generations of children who were born in surplus or deficit, and here's the rub: for boys, their *grandfather* had the ability to shave thirty-two years off their average life span, even after other socioeconomic factors were taken into account, if he had lived through a boom year with plenty of food. These grandfathers were passing down their genes, sure, but their genes were already set in stone when they experienced famine. What the study, published in the *Journal of Medical Genetics*, revealed was that they were also passing down their *experiences*. Incredibly, when the study was expanded, the researchers found that grandmothers who had been starved of nutrients while in the womb passed on a significantly greater risk of early death to their granddaughters.

Once upon a time this was a heresy in science, but the discovery of molecules that express genes has changed the way the world thinks. Childhood experiences, always viewed as character building or destroying, go further than just memories around which a self is formed. These experiences infiltrate the body, too, and stay there for a lifetime and beyond.

A team of US neuroscientists tracked 130 children over three years. They found that those who grew up in disadvantaged households collected more of these epigenetic markers near a single gene called SLC6A4, which helps control levels of the neurochemical serotonin. Brain scans on these children helped connect the dots: more genetic markers were associated with significant levels of activity in the amygdala, one of the oldest structures in the brain, which essentially tells a person when to panic. Over-active amygdalae were precursors to children in the study later reporting high levels of depression. 'These small daily hassles of scraping by are evident in changes that build up and affect children's development,' Duke University's Johnna Schwarz told my friend and reporter John Ross when the research was released.

Columbia University associate professor Kimberley Noble, a developmental cognitive neuroscientist, is at the forefront of an emerging field. Noble led a study of 1099 children to look at the effects of low income during childhood on the brain. The study, published in *Nature Neuroscience* in 2015, was unequivocal. For those who came from few resources, their brain surface area was markedly smaller than that of those from even middle-income families. Importantly, small differences in family income for those poor children were associated with large increases in brain surface area. The same effect was scarcely observed in those with more money. In short, a little money means a lot for the poorest children.

'These relationships were most prominent in regions supporting language, reading, executive functions and spatial skills,' the study concluded. The difference in surface area was as much as 6 per cent, which is the kind of thing a person doesn't notice even if, decades later, they find themselves making inexplicable and poorly reasoned decisions about how to live their life.

Also in 2015, a separate paper published in *JAMA Pediatrics* outlined the effect of poverty on the *volume* of grey matter in the part of the brain associated with cognition and learning. The paper, titled 'Association of child poverty, brain development and academic achievement', showed brain volumes shrank by as much as 20 per cent, and 10 per cent on average. 'Our work suggests that specific brain structures tied to processes critical for learning and educational functioning (e.g., sustained attention, planning, and cognitive flexibility) are vulnerable to the environmental circumstances of poverty, such as stress, limited stimulation, and nutrition,' writes Nicole Hair, the paper's lead author and a researcher with Michigan University's Department of Health Management and Policy. 'If so, it would appear that children's potential for academic success is being reduced at young ages by these circumstances.'

I've never had my brain scanned, though I wonder how much my impulsive and short-sighted life skills owe to the stress of those years from age six.

Kylie, a friend of mine, grew up in similar circumstances to those I knew. But whereas my home was consistent and stable— we were nearly drowning but it was always the same people going under: Mum and her three children—Kylie's home life was more erratic. She can now make Excel spreadsheets for Australia. She is a younger version of what my mum was forced to be, though her dedication comes from a determination never to be in the situation she knew so well as a child. Kylie will happily spend a Friday night talking about finances and budget planning, especially when it comes to her disturbed analysis of my own affairs. 'You are hopeless,' she has said to me about once a month for the duration of our friendship.

When I first moved to Sydney in 2011, I took a $20000 pay cut and my friend Bridie's husband Matt wondered how I would survive. 'It's Rick. He could earn $30000 or $150000 and he would still spend every cent,' Bridie told him. They had observed in me a latent response to my own upbringing. Where Mum worked tirelessly and scrupulously to provide for her children, she went entirely without herself. Our only comfort in childhood came at her own expense.

Perhaps I saw in this unceasing effort no reward. What was the point of all that attention to detail and incredible self-restraint if it moved you nowhere? I'm not poor as an adult, but I have the mind and body of a child who grew up with little and who is sure it can all be taken away. There is a line the breadth of a single human hair that separates my life today from the one I used to know and that my mother still knows. Part of it is unrelated mental illness, but there is, too, a part of me that knows all this effort and all this accumulation of income and career skills could all come to nothing. That is the secret knowledge of every adult who was once a poor child—there is nobody to catch you when it all comes undone.

So what do you do? If you manage to break the cycle, you either become a Kylie or you become me, spending everything you've ever earned to avoid a future you were never truly sure was waiting for you.

I knew more than most eight-year-olds should about the financial pressures their parents are under. I was mature for my age and Mum would confide in me when things got particularly tough. There were more child support reviews than I could fathom and when another crushing adjustment was made, I would share her disbelief. When Dad figured out how to game the system, we got a letter explaining he would pay just $21 a month. 'That's not even a loaf of bread each week for the three of you,' Mum said.

Sometimes she would go on extended monologues about the reviews and the financial stress. When we were good, they were aimed at the injustice of it all, the *system* that kept us where we were. If it was one of us kids causing trouble, however, she would break open like a log fire turned to embers. A light left on, the TV blaring into the night, or if we forgot to turn our fan off when we went to school—her face would shine red and spittle would shoot out. 'Do you want to be kicked out into the gutter? Because that is what'll happen if you kids don't start helping me,' she would scream.

The gutter wasn't just a mother's literary device. It was a real place that we were kept from by sheer will and effort alone. Other families cut the end-of-year holiday when times were rough, but we had nowhere left for the scalpel to run. Mum has never had a credit card, nor any payday loans. She has never smoked, and aside from the odd lotto ticket or scratchie from the newsagent she does not gamble. It is entirely possible I have consumed more rum and Cokes in a single weekend than all the alcohol she has consumed in her lifetime. Still, we had no money.

It takes more time to be poor than it does to have rich or even mid-range incomes. This includes the working poor, a segment of poverty that has been growing since the turn of the millennium. A Grattan Institute report from 2014 shows that in some of Melbourne's outer suburbs, for instance, just 10 per cent of jobs are available a 45-minute, one-way drive from a person's home. The figure is about the same in Brisbane. Switch to public transport, however, and that proportion of jobs only becomes accessible within an hour's travel time. The same report shows that both housing wealth and income wealth grew more quickly in suburbs close to the inner city.

In many nuclear families today, both parents need to work to make ends meet, if soaring childcare costs allow it. A poverty of time and of money is a many-tentacled malady, but I have experienced it most in relation to food. There are products made for people in such conditions and they tend to come frozen. Mum had a repertoire of stews, apricot chickens, mince and cheap veal schnitzels, but as often as not we'd eat fish fingers, pizza pockets, pop tarts, frozen chips and nuggets for dinner and breakfast. When we went to town, KFC and McDonald's were considered a treat but also cheap enough to feed a family of four and still be considered a night out. The cost of healthy, fresh food as a proportion of income in Australia is routinely above 30 per cent in Queensland, and in some parts of Tasmania it's almost 50 per cent for a couple on welfare with children, according to state-based studies.

Mum would often bake the most wonderful desserts but meal-times were workhorse routines. As for me, like many young men, I made spaghetti bolognaise and only spagbol for most of my twenties. It wasn't even a refined version. Mince in pan, spaghetti in saucepan, tomato sauce on top. I'd never cooked before I moved out of home, certainly never with fresh produce. When I was nineteen I decided to branch out a little and bought some mushrooms to go with a steak I was going to cook. For reasons not entirely clear, I put the mushroom in a frying pan and it eventually transformed into a kind of limp, lifeless smudge on the plate.

These are habits that have so far taken me more than a decade to bend or break. Progress was slow, but I slowly started eating foods that had never once been a part of my life. Sushi, Indian, Vietnamese, Thai. They all had flavours I didn't think foods were supposed to have, or even could have. This also led to an embracing of chilli instead of a beginner's tragic miscalculation.

When I covered the Hobart bureau for *The Australian*, I flew Mum down to visit for the week and we spent most nights picking our way through the pubs. 'I just want something simple, darl,' she told me. We might have eaten every chicken parmi in the city. On Bruny Island we stayed at a beach house and I bought some locally produced pork sausages and apples that I endeavoured to caramelise with a degree of success bordering on late-in-life Napoleonic. I never said it to Mum then, but I knew even this flight of edible whimsy was a luxury. I could afford to buy the apples even though we technically didn't need them, and the boutique sausages (which any normal butcher in the 1990s would have rightly laughed at), and, more importantly, I had the abundance of fallow in my own mind to give it a go.

Most single parents I know or have interviewed for my reporting are not out there each night plating up masterpieces with 'hero' ingredients. A pork cutlet should not be a hero unless it has rescued a family of five from churning surf.

While poverty often comes with a litany of other conditions, such as family breakdown, poor nutrition and violence, Kimberley Noble, who runs the Neurocognition, Early Experience and Development Lab at Columbia University, has set out to prove that poverty itself can change the brain. Writing in *Scientific American*, Noble brings together a field of studies in advance of her own five-year opus, which should settle the question for now. Not only might such changes affect the brain, they might be hardwired in early.

'This finding is consistent with work from other labs suggesting that adversity can, in some cases, accelerate brain maturation—in essence, causing a young child's brain to "grow up" more quickly,' Noble writes. 'The rapid reduction of cortical thickness suggests that many poor children's brains may lack "plasticity"—an ability to change in structure to accommodate the essential learning that takes place during childhood and adolescence.'

One of the most interesting stories I've worked on in my career as a journalist was when, in 2014, I interviewed researchers from the Brotherhood of St Laurence who had been tracking 167 babies born in 1990 and their families to study the effects of low income on their lives. The study sprang up specifically in 1990 because, three years earlier (in the year I was born), prime minister Bob Hawke announced no Australian child would live in poverty.

'One thing I really wanted to look at was, to what extent did the cost of existing prohibit these young people from really engaging productively in work, education and life?' lead author and senior researcher with the brotherhood, Janet Taylor, told me. Taylor, who is also an honorary senior fellow and works in the school of social and political sciences at the University of Melbourne, said the study uncovered 'patterns of stressors on families on low incomes that are intense and very different to those suffered by people who have more stable and better incomes. But we've found resilience as well: children born to disadvantaged circumstances who have flourished.'

The rise in the value of social security payments has done little to offset the span of inequality. Welfare lowered the inequality of equivalised market income by 28 per cent in 1993–94 but by only 23 per cent in 2009–10. As the working poor take flight, the welfare system is doing less and less to close the gap for which it was once designed.

I have never been ashamed of my upbringing. Rather, there is pride. I am proud especially of my mother's efforts to shepherd me and my brother and sister into the world. There is anger, too, though not at us. It's directed at a system that overwhelmingly keeps people in their place.

When I was in high school, Mum made it clear that there were no shortcuts. 'You will have to work harder for everything you ever need,' she told me. 'Nobody else is going to do the work for you.' There is a handy resilience forged under such conditions, one that made me a better employee. I had no connections, no networks, no family even in the big cities where I would end up working. There was only Mum, back home in her little Queenslander she managed to buy in 2000.

More dumb luck, really. We had been renting, always renting, when the owner of that home got sick of having it on the market for more than $100 000. She liked my mum because Deb paid her rent on time and looked after the place. The owner dropped the price to about $80 000 and, with the $7000 first homeowner's grant, Mum secured a home loan. It was the most the bank would allow her but it was just enough. It's home.

'That's where I sit and do my thinking,' she says, pointing at a log in the garden when I am home one year.

'Like Socrates?'

'No, like me.'

The lavender abuts the strawberries. It's here she first found the little bearded dragon with a kink in his tail. He arrived in her life that way; no powerful backstory, no explanation for it. Just a big, crooked tail shaped like a meat hook.

'That's where the lizard is. He's on sabbatical,' she says.

'Are you sure he's not dead?'

Mum pauses, lost in herself. 'I hope not. He was doing so well.'

Today my sister Lauryn and I support Mum when she needs it. She takes care of herself and hates asking for money but when she does, we have it. If it is the start of the pay month I will slip her an extra $50 or $100 on top of the bills so she can go out and treat herself. Usually, that involves a contribution to some home-improvement project which has been done necessarily in stages.

On my last visit home we went up to the hardware store and I bought her a bucket of undercoat and primer paint for her new fence, then we went out into the sun with our rollers and went to work. It felt insignificant, this little token of my appreciation. I grew tired after working for an hour and a bit and she let me have a smoke in the shade while she kept dabbing away at the blank posts, always working.

'You had enough darl,' she said from beneath her cap.

The sun was quite bright.

CHAPTER 6

ENTANGLEMENT

In a moment of motherly affection rare at the time, Deb decided to drop off some mail to my older brother, who had recently moved out, again. Along with the stack of letters, mostly fines and duty lawyer legal advice, she'd picked up one of Toby's favourite treats and was standing in his driveway ready to deliver. Though she later conceded it was odd, Mum didn't think too much about the unusual number of cars parked near the home and inside the yard that day, which is how she came to be standing in the middle of a drug raid with a bottle of iced coffee and several envelopes.

When a female police officer shone a light in her face, Mum must have looked like an inmate caught between duelling prison searchlights in one of those old-time cartoons.

'Who are you?' the officer asked.

'Only his mother,' Mum cried out feebly from the driveway. 'I'm just delivering his mail.'

I asked Mum once if she had ever broken the law. She paused for a considerable period of time while she assessed what I presumed to be a secret history that none of us had ever heard. 'I was probably drunk in public once,' she ventured. It was this innocence that apparently compelled the policewoman to believe her. Mum relinquished the letters and, her duties over, climbed back in her car and beat a swift retreat. 'I never even got to give him the iced coffee,' she said later.

Deborah Morton's driving record was immaculate. She had never lied on a tax return, never inflated her deductions, or taken sick days when she wasn't sick. She believed, even then in her mid-fifties, that many things more than were actually enshrined in law were illegal. Which accounts for how—apart from a brief flirtation with becoming a detective when she was younger, cruelled on account of her short stature—Mum's life had only once before crossed paths with the law. Hers was an existence of such stultifying devotion to the rule of law and honesty that Catholic orders might have sprung up in her honour had she been more visible.

Despite the influence of alcohol in our lives, to us, drug addiction was something that happened to other people. The kind you read about in the papers. The people whose kids were given up to the foster care system because they tried to medicate their own traumas. And then their kids, abandoned for other substances, went on to do the same. My brother's spiral into drug abuse and lawlessness was slow and wide, at first, and telegraphed none of what lay ahead.

Based on statistics alone, even as a snow-haired young boy, Toby was likely to become a heavy drinker and smoker by his late teens. Our father smokes rollies and would often get us to hold the wheel of the car on the open road while he dithered around in his tin of Log Cabin tobacco. He also drank heavily. On one trip back from the pub, my father turned to Mum and complained that he could not fold the pram properly. 'That's because your fucking son is in there,' she screamed at him, noticing my little baby body gallantly holding the pram open.

Researchers would label this binge-drinking. Much of the country would call it 'going out'. In any case, we become our parents to a startling degree, and my brother at the age of nine was more like his dad than any other Morton.

Toby was slender-boned, short and into mischief without pause. He rolled the sleeves of his R.M. Williams shirts up at the elbow, like Dad, and was grading roads in the Caterpillar by age eleven. He went mustering with the jackaroos for weeks at a time while I stayed home with Mum to read books and be in my head. Toby idolised our father and, importantly, our father idolised him. I loved Dad too, though it was never quite the same.

Around the age of five, I waved at Dad as he mounted his horse one day and rode off to muster the beef cattle in the home paddock. He did not wave back or acknowledge me in any way so, quietly, I followed him. With our blue heeler Puppity in tow, I slipped out of the homestead yard and followed my father down to the creek, which had recently flooded and was slick with mud. Dad was on the other side of the creek and still hadn't seen me when I waded into the water and became stuck up to my hips in the thick clay bed. Cattle were moving all around me and I remember the distinct pangs of disappointment when Puppity did not come and rescue me like I assumed all dogs did after watching *Lassie*. I screamed and it was Mum who heard me, all the way back in the homestead kitchen where she was working on that day's lunch for the jackaroos and Dad.

There was never any animosity between Toby and I. He had Dad and I had Mum, an even split of two parents. We were each happy in our own way. When he wasn't being a mini-jackaroo we spent most of our waking hours together. Usually, he was prodding me to do things I would never have done of my own free will, like riding the purple PeeWee 50 motorbike into out-of-bounds areas on the cattle station, and chasing wild animals such as dingoes and pigs. It was Toby who suggested we play with the candles in our room and Toby who told me to stash them under the bed when we heard our father coming upstairs. It was Toby who ran first, prompting me to scamper behind him when the bed caught alight, distracting Dad. It was Toby who suggested, after a long day of hiding, to give ourselves up to Dad. It would ameliorate our sentence, he said. Instead, we each got whacked with the belt-buckle end of Dad's leather belt. Diplomacy had gotten us nowhere, except home in time for dinner.

We did our schooling together in the little home room where the wireless radio was. Here, we worked through schoolbooks sent out in packs for the term from the Charleville School of Distance Education and jumped on the radio for a half-hour lesson with our real teachers there. Occasionally, we had help.

It was our first governess, Alison, who beat Toby across the face with an iron bar. I don't remember it, but I remember the court date and being in a quiet room wondering what was happening. My brother had to give evidence. Mum told him to tell only the truth. When the governess' lawyer said my brother was making it all up, he jumped up and pointed at the lawyer: 'I am not telling lies. My mum told me to tell the truth!'

In my family, you just didn't go around hitting other people's children. But later, there would be no punishment for the emotional injuries of a broken family, no salve for the horror of having been burned, and no courtroom that truly asked: What happened to you?

A paper in the journal *Drug and Alcohol Review* in 2012 suggested that as many as 80 per cent of substance abusers have suffered some form of childhood trauma. In many of these cases, they continued to suffer PTSD. A 2013 University of NSW paper, pulling this and other research together in the Australian context, found childhood trauma in some form in 57 per cent of the general population.

But among cannabis users it was 83 per cent. Some 93 per cent of those who had dangerously used sedatives had experienced childhood trauma, as had 89 per cent of opioid users and 91 per cent of those dependent on amphetamines.

The greatest single category of early trauma these people claimed was being witness to serious injury or death (68 per cent) followed by kidnapping or being physically attacked or threatened. The median age at first trauma? Seven. Government data tells us about 5 per cent of all Australians have a substance use disorder in any twelve-month period. For those aged sixteen to twenty-four, the figure is one in eight. Young men are chained to such disorders at a much higher rate, still.

Toby is at the heart of these statistics. If you had built a boy based only on these findings, it would have been my brother.

When I was in nappies I fell into a pond. It wasn't particularly deep but neither was I. Toby was the only one who saw me plunge into the water and he breezily whipped me out, fist balled around my water-logged nappy. To the young soul, this is how you rescue someone. It is always an act of physical heroism of some description. That's why firefighters, police and paramedics always seem so *capable*. It never occurred to me as a boy that there were other, more difficult ways to rescue someone. A single question would consume my adult life: How do you save a mind?

Toby started using marijuana in high school, like many teenagers in the late 1990s and early 2000s. There are few other things to do in regional Queensland. He was still recovering from his burns when he began high school but made friends easily enough, though in a different crowd to me. Where his mates rode dirt bikes and skateboards, mine played computer games. We rarely crossed over but, when we did, the results were not ideal. Around 2002 I went down to the skatepark to film one of my brother's new moves—

'the axe murderer', he called it—and I later spliced the footage together with a song I thought he and his friends would enjoy. The American singer Pink's hit 'Just Like a Pill' was not, I later discovered, the kind of edgy musical accompaniment demanded by the skatepark crowd.

He and I have always been fundamentally different creatures. But in the same way that a suckerfish can use a shark, and the shark can use a suckerfish, we existed together in a state of symbiosis. I helped him with his school assignments and he was cool enough to act as a bulldozer for me in high school, lending me a certain credibility with the tough kids I could never have hoped to build on my own. I was a boy, in the sense that when my brother leaned into a steer carcass and cut out its bladder, I would join in the game of soccer that followed, piss flying out the end of the organ like a balloon filled with Gatorade. But I would never entirely *give* myself to the game because the only game I was playing was to try to fit in, and that absorbed all the energy I had to offer. Toby had a surplus of energy.

We were, for so many years, the only children we knew and got to hang out with. For the seven years before my sister Lauryn was born, it was just him and me. Something in that arrangement meant we were tethered together, through experiences shared and dissimilar. While he burned, I looked over the edge of the pit and saw it all. Our Dad left us both, and our newborn sister. He was straight, I was gay. He was good at sport, I was into books. For the first years we were alive he owned his world and I felt uncomfortable in it. Then he was ripped away from everything he knew. He lost his best friend, Dad, and we moved to Boonah, a town with only 3000 people but one we saw as positively cosmopolitan compared with the cattle station. In his unhappiness, like so many of us, he turned to drugs.

At first, it was recreational, and he continued part-time work during school as an apprentice carpenter. Later, when he lost his licence for speeding, Mum would rise at five each morning and drive him the hour round-trip to work and do the same in the afternoon after she finished at the school. She performed this same monotonous expression of a mother's love for three months. When he turned eighteen, he received an $80 000 compensation payout for his injuries. He bought me a $4000 desktop computer with all the latest features and himself a brand new ute, which he tricked up with thousands of dollars of extras. Returning over New Year's from Sydney—where, we later learned, he had been running drugs—he flipped the ute end-over-end on the highway.

As my brother's drug use, and dealing, increased, mine began. One night in the late 2000s my brother told me he was going to The Beat, an iconic queer nightclub in Brisbane, and I told him I would also be there. We were both mildly curious, each realising we were approaching confirmation of the thing about the other we had long suspected. That was this: I was gay and my brother was a small-time drug dealer. The Beat was fertile ground for drug dealers, one of the few reasons straight men ever wandered inside. It was not the melting pot sexuality rights activists had imagined but it was a useful first step.

I arranged to buy three ecstasy pills from him and then told him I was gay. 'I know,' he said, laughing. Synthetic emotional transaction completed, we parted ways to indulge our respective dives into oblivion. And then he went to prison for being part of an elaborate ecstasy operation in Brisbane's Fortitude Valley.

In those dark years of my early twenties I was grappling with my own latent infestations of the soul. I was scared, living half a lie, and my career had detonated. My own drug use was becoming problematic. Even so, I made sure I never had the contact number of a dealer and never actively sought them out. I frequently made bad decisions when I was around drugs but they didn't carry on into the next day. I was firmly in the experimentation phase. My drinking problem was more serious.

Here's something that is easy to forget. All drugs, both legal and illegal, work because our bodies produce precisely the same chemicals. Because we produce those chemicals or constituent elements, we have receptors for them, which means we can jam them in artificially from the outside, if we so wish. And many Australians wish. This fact is often cited as reason enough to gobble whatever we like. Certainly, it is often used by people like me who dabbled without ever tumbling down the ravine into full-blown addiction.

Perhaps it was guilt over this that stopped me from visiting my brother in jail. He was inside for three months—a short stay, all things considered—and I couldn't bring myself to see him. Why him and not me? Were his horrors greater than mine? These questions consumed my waking hours and, at some level, I couldn't escape the fatalism of it all.

One of the most bizarre elements of quantum mechanics, the scientific theory that popped up early last century to explain the behaviour of particles on the smallest of scales, is entanglement. It's so weird and alien to our senses that Einstein called it 'spooky action'. It seems like some fancy trick but while we cannot fully explain it, it has been measured countless times in carefully controlled experiments. It is real.

Take one particle, a photon, and entangle it with another. Fling them out into the far reaches of space and then measure them. These photons, once so alike, can be at the ends of the very universe itself and still be inextricably linked. Measure one and the other reacts instantly. Instantly. Nothing in this world is meant to overtake the speed of light, save for the expansion of the fabric of the universe itself, and yet, something strange happens between these two particles. A message, perhaps. Something is transmitted between them faster than light. And they turn and turn out there in the vast inkwell of space.

I began to see my brother's and my life as the effect of some cosmic process. His suffering was my advance. As he grew weaker, I grew stronger. He went to jail and I escaped punishment for my own misdemeanours.

When Toby was released he was caught in a state-sanctioned window of clarity. The sobriety tests kept him clear of drug use for a little while. Toby was back with us, having shaken the rain off at the door. He went back to work, got another girlfriend with three kids—his first adult girlfriend had also had three kids. I called them his instant families: just add water. Part of this was true, of course. He relished playing the not-so-old father role for the young children, especially the boys. Especially young Marcus, who was nine. Marcus idolised him and my brother loved him, genuinely. Marcus had blond hair, almost white, just like Toby when he was nine. Marcus didn't have a father, either.

Toby bought the kids toys and played rough, pretending to fight them. Our dad did that too. It always bothered me but then I wasn't a real boy. Not really, not to him. My brother lapped it up. He liked playing with the risk of being hurt. That was tough. Being emotionally hurt was never part of the bargain. It's the Faustian drama that punctures the lives of anybody who loves.

It was painful to watch him play-acting the childhood he was denied, this time as the father figure. He borrowed from the best things about Dad and discarded the rest. He was good at it and you could see in him, somewhere behind the eyes, that this, this was what he wanted. The worthwhile life. He did everything else because he couldn't fully inhabit this life, didn't know how. Wasn't taught how.

Around the 1980s, court systems across Australia began implementing a range of diversionary programs for drug offences.

The programs evolved over time and in Queensland, where we lived, they applied only to first-time offenders. If you'd been offered a diversion before there wouldn't be another. Here and in other states, judges could take into account drug and alcohol diversion attendance in recording the conviction or, more typically, in deciding the sentence. For many, this became a way of avoiding jail. Rarely did the programs treat the serious underlying issues, even when they mandated a cursory three counselling sessions.

In a 2015 Australian Institute of Criminology round-up of court-based diversion programs around the nation, the word 'trauma' is not mentioned once. We are long past the point of finding excuses for Toby, and others like him, but the truth of the matter is that a failure to understand why people become dependent drug users is a serious failure of policy. The court systems have long dealt assiduously with trauma in relation to victims of crime, as is right and proper. But many offenders have optimistically been given re-education pamphlets and left, again, to their own devices in the community.

The words of the warden of the Rhode Island Department of Corrections, in a work cited by the Law Institute of Victoria in an October 2016 report, say it too well: 'Most, if not all, situations of conflict and harm involve questions of justice and injustice, and situations of injustice frequently involve trauma.'

When my brother's relationship eventually failed, just like the one before, after the fighting again got too much, he turned to one of the most frightening drugs of all: ice. A few years before this moment, I'd heard about ice—methamphetamines in crystal form—for the first time. I was a cadet journalist on the Gold Coast. I was all of eighteen, perched in the police scanner room where we spent night shifts listening to emergency radio broadcasts from the same heroes I'd once imagined rescuing people. And they did, often, but this also revealed to me the vast boundaries of substance abuse and the violence that so often comes with it. Night after night, call after call. Women beaten by their partners. Men beaten and stabbed and shot at by other men chasing drug debts. 504. That was code for a mental patient, often used by the cops when a person was in psychosis and often because of drugs.

But one call stood out in an ocean of insanity. A man, with a history of using ice, cut his own balls off with boltcutters. He was high at the time, though the scanner did not divulge on what, and there he went and castrated himself. It's not useful agonising over the mechanics except to say the man was probably in psychosis—in such a state that the usual rules of polite society, such as not assaulting people or dispensing with your testes, do not apply.

In the past decade a litany of scientific studies have been conducted into the effects of methamphetamine use on executive function in the brain. The results are varied but the most recent, presented by Tong-Yu Wang and others in the *Americal Journal of Addictions* in 2017, show a significant link between the use of ice and a long-term decline in cognitive functions. These are the types of functions that help ordinary people make rational decisions with minimal risk. Crucially, the research shows persistent effects even among users who have gone off the drug for long periods of time. Whether the degradation is permanent or not, nobody knows.

Here's the kicker: there is evidence that the kind of talk and cognitive behaviour therapy used on people to treat addiction and the underlying causes loses its effect on those whose brains have been transfigured by methamphetamine. Put simply, missed opportunities at the earliest stages of drug use are likely to stay missed. The drug-addled mind loses the chance to right itself the longer an individual marches on into a chemical nowhere-land.

Toby began using ice around 2013. We know this because for the first time in his life he became violent and threatening towards my mother, and towards Lauryn, who was still living at home and studying to become a midwife. If Toby had introduced himself to the court system, he dragged us in, too, in what became a desperate bid to keep him away.

Toby would use all night then go out into the mountains with friends to collect pieces of wood and 'be with nature'. He told us the red-bellied black snakes couldn't hurt him because he was one of them. There is a reason you've never seen a professional snake-handler on the job while cooked on ice. Part of me wanted him to be bitten.

Those who encouraged him spoke often of everyone else being 'sheep' and 'asleep', as if the drugs were the only way to have any-body wake up. They saw their newly acquired mental states as being on a higher plane, a portal to awareness. How spurious those claims seemed for the rest of us, destined to watch the users plunge into barely functional stasis. Take the speed, the ice, burn all night, dry out, search for more. My brother said he had never been happier. He stopped working. He even stopped pretending to work, such that his dole was eventually cut off. But when the drugs failed him, or his stash ran out, he would fly into a rage. He threatened to hit my mum and punched my sister in the face. He pulled the phone out of the wall when they went to call the police. This happened again and again.

I have never felt rage like I did in the moment I first found out this had happened. Mum was already ill from the stress of it all, an anxious person beaten down by such an unfathomable set of circumstances. And he had scared her, frightened her. She had never done anything but try to love out the dark in him. Anger lived beneath my skin.

There are two ways a person can get a domestic violence order in Queensland. The police can initiate one, but by their own admission in our case, Toby would have had to be practically in the act of killing or assaulting us before they could move in. In the country town where we lived, though the police were professional and helpful, they were not rostered on at all hours. When the country officers were not on, the city cops had to come from more than half-an-hour away in Ipswich.

The alternative is through the court system, which is laborious and takes time. Mum went once and endured what was to her an agonising and demeaning process. Though it exists for a purpose, my brother was given the right to answer the notice before it was served.

In Victoria, where data on family violence is the most complete of any state or territory, police recorded almost 75 000 incidents in that category in 2015. An analysis of their books suggests about three-quarters of the perpetrators are recidivists. They come back again and again and again in the numbers. The state's crime statistics body, drawing on established research, notes: 'Perpetrator unemployment, residential instability, low socio-economic status, living in a socio-economically disadvantaged neighbourhood and lower levels of educational attainment in the neighbourhood have all been shown to be risk factors for domestic violence recidivism.'

The rates are much higher in regional areas, away from the glare of the capital cities. Though my brother finished high school, at our insistence, our family could again be built from the statistics.

None of this is an argument for destiny, of course, though looking back we ought not have been surprised about where we had ended up. In many ways, the path before us was rigged. That Mum had suffered emotional, financial and physical abuse at the hands of our father for so many years was tragedy enough. But here, at the other end of her life, she lived in fear of her son. I will never be able to understand the internal cataclysm of a mother facing this in her own son. It was unfair, I thought, that she must endure this now after two decades of daily battles for survival.

When the first violence order had been served, Toby came around to the house screaming one day, and cowardly the very next, stunted by the threat of jail. Mum did not report him on the second breach, though he was not supposed to enter the property. I told her over the phone that it was important to stay firm, lest any future transgressions be looked on unfavourably because she selectively enforced the terms of the order. In spite of it all, she was caught between the pincer movement of her own maternal instincts and her dread. On the other end of the line was a shattered woman: 'I know, Rick. But I just can't fight it anymore. I'm exhausted. They want me to go to court. I can't do it anymore.'

This is the first and only time I have ever heard my mum admit defeat. Not once before, when the money ran out, when thieves turned off the power in our housing commission home, when she lodged her tenth child support review, when my brother went to jail, when we were terrible children, when the phone was cut off because the bill hadn't been paid. Nothing had stopped her. She was granite to the elements. And they were harsh elements. They were unfair elements. She stood against them.

Now, she was tired. It broke me to hear it.

Toby moved out again, but when he came whimpering back, Mum let him stay, underneath the Queenslander in which she lived. He turned the concrete expanse into something resembling a psychedelic junkyard. He took up painting, calling himself Shroomy and largely rendering mushrooms in the same neon-bright colours he had spray-painted on the walls. At the age of thirty he broke every one of the rules Mum had set for him. No friends were allowed on her property, no drugs were to be consumed on her property, no loud music late at night. He cared for none of it and milked her kindness time and time again. His parade of drug-addicted friends came around at all hours, stayed the night, frightened Mum in the dark when she came downstairs in the dead of night to take the dogs outside.

By this point, Mum was living on her own. My sister now lived seven hours north in Gladstone, while I lived ten hours south in Sydney. In every way, our now lifelong poverty informed everything about how we dealt with Mum's new regime of fear and violence at home. We might have checked Toby into a rehab centre but we didn't have the money. If we had had the money, such services were voluntary and there was no guarantee they would work. Places around Australia for ice addiction in particular were—and still are—limited. On occasion, it has been cheaper for families to fly to South-East Asia than to try the options at home.

The average cost of private rehabilitation in Australia for people hooked on ice and other illicit substances is about $20 000. Even for those who can afford the treatment, the outcomes vary wildly. Take the now famous case of the daughter of former NSW premier Neville Wran. Harriet was twenty-six when she faced a murder charge, for which she was later acquitted, after getting hooked on the drug ice and falling into relationships with users in Sydney's 'underworld'. Her mother Jill twice paid for her to attend clinics: once in Queensland, where she began a relationship with another addict, and again in the Sydney beachside suburb of Clovelly, where she later began using ice with others who were also trying to get clean.

Harriet had gone to two of Sydney's most exclusive girls' schools and her mother was a paid-up member of the city's literature and arts scene. What chance do those with fewer means really stand in the face of such an insidious and belligerent addiction?

In 2016, I interviewed Kelli Pfeiffer, whose son Blake, then a teenager, had become hooked on ice. Though she fought to get him clean she ran into the blockade that is an inadequate system of detoxification and rehab centres. To go to rehab you must detox first, but with ice this can take ten to eighteen days—assuming a person can get a place in a detox centre or rehab outfit when they are often guarded by strict eligibility criteria. In Kelli's case, her son, at age seventeen, was either too young or too old. The windows of opportunity that could land someone in rehabilitation are opened and shut in a dizzying sequence. Only those who manage to make them line up gain any solace at all.

'Each time Blake found himself in that situation where he did want to get off drugs, it was only fleeting,' she says. 'At first he would always say yes, so I'd make the connections to get him into rehab and by that stage he had changed his mind and he was gone. It would be months in between visits.'

Kelli's own GP in Rockhampton took the extraordinary step of trying to detox Blake at home, dropping in to supervise the effort over one week. When this was done, Kelli set off on a 21-day road trip without having locked in a rehab place, in the desperate hope one would become available. 'I kept thinking about driving into oncoming traffic, seeing all those trucks drive past,' she says. 'The only question was which truck driver did I want to kill and take with us.'

Blake was eventually accepted as a student at the Triple Care Farm south of Sydney, which is run by the national charity Mission Australia and takes about 100 young people aged sixteen to twenty-four each year. The farm is one of the most successful programs of its type in Australia. But it does not take students who have not detoxed, nor does it help those with serious, daily drug habits. In other words, it does not take adults like my brother.

During my weekly chats with Mum, I took to subjecting our crisis to trademark dark humour. It was important, down there in the well, to know how to laugh. Laughter, I figured, told us which way was up, even in the absence of light.

Mum had distracted herself with a family of possums that had moved into the roof cavity of her home. She was not enamoured with the possums but, rather, wanted to get rid of them because they kept her up at night. Here she was, wedged between the marsupials above her and her son below. When one of the baby possums grew up and was banished from the territory, I told Mum the animals had had more success getting their children to move out of home than she had.

The first police raid of my mother's house was a surprise. Two officers knocked on the front door and were shown downstairs. Their names, improbably, were Leather and Patch and they took detailed notes, though they found little of consequence except for an ice pipe. Mum was ashamed and in tears, but she later took particular offence to their description of the property, which noted the yard fence was 'rundown and in need of repair'. She said to me: 'It's being repaired Rick. Why'd they have to put that in there?'

Over the Christmas period Toby began making the ice pipes himself, presumably as a value-add to his business selling drugs. While he beavered away downstairs, Mum was upstairs cross-stitching her annual festive reindeers that she would mail out to my sister and me. The juxtaposition was lost on none of us. 'Now how the hell did he learn glassblowing, that's what I'd like to know,' Mum said. 'It's a skill!'

We called the police to have them raid the house once more, in an attempt to remove Toby. They raided the home on one more occasion, too, though without us having to ask. Our great hope, degraded though it was, was that he would be packed off to jail again. After years of serious battles, jail seemed like the only plausible option to take him from our hands and break the circuit of his drug use.

That jail ever became a solution would once have horrified me. Toby's first stint many years previous offered punishment for his crimes but came so long after the crimes themselves that it interrupted a brief period where he had managed to right himself and get back to work. The justice system moves so slowly and sweeps all before it.

Criminal courts in most states are groaning under the weight of wrongdoing. Reports from the Productivity Commission show that many of these court systems are operating above capacity. In Queensland, 33 per cent of cases in the Magistrates Court system are more than six months old, the highest percentage in the country. More than 14 per cent have lasted for longer than a year, topped only by 15 per cent of cases in the Northern Territory. In the NSW and South Australian District/County Court systems, one-quarter of all cases had dragged on for more than a year as at June 2016. The figures aren't much better in other states and territories. In NSW, Queensland, South Australia, Tasmania and the ACT, cases are being lodged faster than the old ones can be finalised and cleared.

Jails, too, are overcrowded. Nationally, all prisons are running at 111 per cent of their design capacity. Figures are slightly below capacity for open facilities but stand at 115 per cent for secure ones; in NSW, secure facilities are booked to more than 120 per cent of their design. In these prisons, fewer than 40 per cent of inmates are enrolled in some kind of education and training. Under 80 per cent of prisoners are employed while behind bars. An average of 37 000 prisoners are held in custody every day, excluding those in periodic detention. It costs the states and territories about $300 per prisoner per day to keep them locked up.

My family has never held the belief that prison would fix my brother. Or any inmate, for that matter. While they have an obvious community safety function, prisons are largely wasted opportunities, storing offenders at great cost without changing them or treating them, and releasing them again to continue an infernal cycle. That lack of belief was not to be challenged when the police again came for Toby. Like the first time, they found only an ice pipe which, even in light of his record, was not enough to put him away. Even when he crashed his car into a power pole, he received only a warning.

Mum tried to evict him but because he paid no rent and was her son, she had none of the rights traditionally available to a landlord. Though he was abusive and threatened her while high, another meeting with the police about a domestic violence order went nowhere.

Mum said to me later: 'I told the officer I was ready to kill him [Toby] and he said, "I don't want to hear any more." But I said to him, "I don't have a gun, I don't have a knife."'

That's not ideal, I told her, reminding Mum that we were trying to get a DVO against our brother, not convince the cops to grant one against her.

'Well, either way he's going to leave the house,' she said.

Though we'd long given up wondering what an escalation in the situation would look like, things began spinning out of control when a local man, Carl King, began chasing Toby for a debt, likely drug-related. Toby told him he had a 'gay brother in Melbourne' who was going to take care of the debt. I had heard of no such arrangement, which was surprising given I was apparently the one who was going to square the ledger. The man contacted me by Facebook and told me he had mates in a Victorian bikie gang who could come round and collect the money. 'All good, I've got your address,' he said. Thankfully, I was just days away from moving back to Sydney after a one-year stint in the southern city.

My brother had shown with breathtaking frequency how willing he was to involve the wider family, especially Mum, in his habits. I had no intention of paying his debt for him. I wrote back to Carl and told him these were not my problems and that normal people, when they claim something has been stolen from them, report it to the police. The ensuing tirade of homophobic abuse included such all-stars as 'fucken handbag' and 'what you're doing is wrong and against nature' and 'fucken aids spreading germ'.

Carl would prove to be insatiable. A week after our exchange he turned up at my mum's house and broke through her fence before chasing my brother through the yard with an axe. Toby's very presence at the house, as we had forewarned, endangered my family. A few days after the axe incident, a driver lost control and ploughed through the fence. That poor fence—it was, again, rundown and in need of repair.

Ice, more than any other illegal drug, breaks communities wide open. Figures released by the Queensland Minister for Child Safety in April 2017 showed that half the children in state care were there because their parents used ice. Whatever our own experience, I knew thousands of others had it worse than us. We had glimpsed the panic and terror of an ice epidemic through which others, especially children, had already been destroyed.

On one assignment for work in 2015, I ended up in Walgett, in far north-western NSW. Walgett is especially pretty when the canola fields that wrap around the town are in bloom. But there, the twin powers of social and economic forces have disfigured a community once near the heart of a thriving agriculture operation. When seasons were good in the decades prior, the region was flush with work. As technology has advanced, however, much of the itinerant work has been taken either by machines or foreign labour. The impact has been catastrophic.

When I visited, assaults during the two years previous were committed at an averaged rate of more than 2063 per 100 000 people—the highest rate in the state—and the region was racked by sexual assaults, alcohol and drug abuse, property damage and theft. Domestic violence, too, had occurred at an astonishing rate: more than 1399 assaults for every 100 000 people. Walgett, you should know, is home to just 6107 people these days, down from 6454 in the 2011 Census. Those who leave the town tend to be non-Indigenous, while those who arrive tend to be Aboriginal people from more remote locations. In this segregated town, almost half of the Indigenous population is unemployed.

When I began talking to parents in the area, they told me horrifying stories about precisely how the ice epidemic took hold. Dealers offer free hits to anyone who will take them, including boys and girls, knowing full well the high is so euphoric that first-time users will be back for more. That's when they make their money. Like all good businessmen and women, they know how to market the product.

Though methamphetamine use has remained relatively stable over the past decade, the fraying of regional towns in particular has been due to a sudden switch between the type used, from speed to the incredibly potent ice. In this leap the damage was done. Ice users are more dangerous on account of the binges. Typical users can mainline the drug for six days straight with little or even no sleep. Psychosis is common, and when hospital admissions are made, police are often required to subdue patients.

Unlike in the cities, residents of small country towns are fully exposed to the decay of their communities and this, to some degree, plays into the arc of political influence. When parties talk tough on drugs and crime, it's because people in these towns and suburbs have seen the chaos firsthand, whether they wanted to be a part of it or not. People like my mother. These are the ordinary Australians who do not live in suburbs kept 'clean' by house prices or poor public transport access.

Even in my job as a journalist covering these issues and the attendant social malaise, the full force of the devastation at the nucleus of towns and families could never have been apparent. Empathy only takes a person so far. I live, these days, in an inner-Sydney apartment and see almost none of this myself. In Surry Hills, where I work, I cross paths with the occasional heroin user injecting in the street, and that would be the extent of my immersion in addiction were it not for the fall of my brother.

Obliviousness, in this case, is a remarkable state of being, one in which many Australians live. While outrage is stoked when the federal government floats trialling the drug-testing of welfare users, it resonates because other people living in proximity to drug users have seen them fritter away entire dole cheques on their habit. I've seen it with Toby. Though my family was saved by the safety net—a single parent payment and family benefits—we've witnessed the way in which a welfare payment can support a habit and nothing else. And that this happens should surprise no-one. There are more than 700 000 people on the dole in Australia and in 2016 almost three-quarters of them had been on the payment for more than a year. Some have been on unemployment benefits since the first day the new allowance was introduced in the early 1990s.

But for every individual who takes a benefit without fair cause there are two or three who desperately need it to live, find work and feed themselves. Even then there is consensus across business and community groups that the payment rate is no longer enough to do all of these things well. As much as I once wished they would cut my brother's payment off for good—and they did temporarily when he missed enough appointments—I knew that any such policy blueprint would wind up catching the desperately poor who have not done the wrong thing.

Watching any government attempt to be hyper-specific in a welfare crackdown is like watching a hydraulic press attempt to make lasagne. There is no such thing as a light touch here. Political outfits like One Nation and the Coalition would have us believe the drug-testing of welfare recipients is about helping these users instead of just cutting the payments off. The reality is far more nuanced, of course, and referrals to treatment services mean little when the services themselves are poorly designed and leak patients like a sieve. An addict's motivation is not bleeding the taxpayer dry. It is simply a pursuit of another high by the most available means. Robbed of one, they turn elsewhere.

There comes a time amid the rush of addiction when the closest family members must give up, for their own survival. After a decade of loving Toby and trying to help him be in the world, our efforts turned to grief. We grieved as if we had already lost him, as if he had died. Those seemed, at this late stage, the only options anyhow. Jail or death. Our only relief, totally diminished, was that he had not fathered children of his own.

Toby did have one girlfriend who he tried to help. Even in the fog of his disease he had an outsized notion of trying to help those fallen beside him. Few had the capacity or desire to return the favours, or even the spirit of them, but he pushed on nevertheless. His girlfriend lived in nearby Ipswich, cut off from us by a total absence of public transport. Her fifteen-month-old son was run over and killed in her driveway by a worker from the Queensland Department of Child Safety.

There seemed so little hope in Toby's circle. His friends Beetle and Scott and Fat Boy abused drugs and alcohol, mourned the children they neglected in waking hours and begged for justice when things went wrong. Everything was interconnected and the smallest things helped stoke the largest scales of their despair. Still, I was worn out and was forced to allocate all my reserves of concern to my mother, who was slowly being eroded by her oldest son. She had stopped sleeping well and the stress was taking its toll on her health. Ultimately, there would be more pressing worries.

On a trip home in July 2017, I was ensconced in the warmth of the living room while Mum and I watched one of her favourite movies, *Bridget Jones's Baby*. By most measures it was a stunningly normal Saturday night. I had bought a tin of primer for Mum's new fence earlier that day and we had spent the mild winter's afternoon applying the coat with rollers. Both of us were exhausted when we heard the yelling downstairs. Toby, who was on a rare trip upstairs baking a cake, raced to the back door, as did Mum. The yelling intensified, so I joined them.

Jason Moore, a friend of Toby's better known as Fat Boy, had stormed the yard and ducked under the house with a golf club, where he proceeded to attack Scott, who was watching television there. In the fury, the club snapped and Jason plunged the severed rod into Scott's neck, just below his left ear. Scott didn't make a sound until Jason bolted, when he wandered outside on to the pavers, hand gripping his neck, and said, half wail, half matter of fact, 'Toby, he's stabbed me.' He then cried 'I need an ambulance' as he fell to his knees and lay down on the brickwork. Blood gushed from the wound and glistened in the security lighting.

I was already on the phone to the ambulance, but there was no time to wait for them. Scott had sung out again, his voice coated in fear: 'I can't feel the left side of my face.' While Mum called the police, Toby bundled Scott into a car and drove the one-minute trip to the local hospital. He returned immediately to abuse us for calling the police and spent the next ten minutes rummaging around under the house for anything incriminating before preparing to do a runner.

'Why'd you have to call the cops? They just make everything worse,' he said. There he went again, travelling the well-worn rut of the addict and caring only about his own circumstances. He'd abandoned his mate at the hospital where another might have stayed and waited on a prognosis, and come home to tear away at us instead. 'Because your fucking mate stabbed your mate in the fucking neck you fuckwit,' I shouted at him. Across the years, I had never raised my voice to my brother as an adult. I had believed, somewhere at an elemental level, that he meant well. It took seeing my mother's reality to fully understand what I could never have understood in my other life.

'Just fuck off Toby. Your friends are dangerous,' I yelled. 'What, and yours aren't?', he shot back. Well, no. It was a bizarre interjection from an addled mind. He took his dog Ziggy and left on foot. Somewhat uncharacteristically, he would call me for my birthday nine months later but that would be the extent of our future contact.

The home where I'd spent high school and where Mum still lived became a crime scene, which the local police sergeant visited to give us his assurances. When he saw me at the door he seemed surprised. 'Rick, how are you mate? I haven't seen you in years,' he said. Such is the way of small towns. In fact, Sergeant Peter Boyce knew more about my brother than I did. It turned out the flurry of violence had happened because Fat Boy was upset about a missing pushbike. The crime scene crew finally packed up and left us at 1 a.m., more than four hours after the stabbing.

Mum and I finished watching *Bridget Jones's Baby*. We were both still on edge when we heard Mum's cat rummaging around in the kitchen. 'Oh, what's Charlie into?', my mother yelled. 'Drugs,'

I laughed. We laughed. Is that what normal people did? Were we normal people? We managed to get an hour's sleep before someone drove past the house and threw two Molotov cocktails at it. The second window-rattling explosion was heard across town. We never did find out who threw them.

This was the life my brother's drug addiction brought Mum, the addiction itself brought by the wounds of family breakdown and physical trauma. One could trace the behaviour of our father back to his father. And so the cycle goes.

The question of what separates my brother and I has haunted me for the better part of a decade. The absolutists will argue on the one hand that he is entirely a prisoner of his circumstances or, on the other, that he is wholeheartedly to blame based on the choices he made along the way. Neither of these positions takes in the shadowland between what is done to us as human beings and what we do after the fact.

Here's an inconvenient truth. Though I may be held up as a worthy product of my upbringing, I did not get here by careful planning. If I made the 'correct' choices, I don't remember making them. Each of us has a threshold for what we can endure in a life. Perhaps if one more thing had stood in my way, I might have imploded. I haven't ended up here, writing this, because I mapped out the right pathway. Rather, I suffered a singular compulsion: to make it out by any means possible. Maybe Toby suffered another motivating force, one whose chief aim was to hide the pain. Maybe that was what survival looked like.

The pre-Columbian Aztecs had a saying for someone who had led a moral life but still fell into trouble: 'It is slippery, it is slick on the Earth.' Western civilisations like to think they stumbled onto philosophy first but the Aztecs had a broader, deeper vision of the Aristotelian mission to lead a good life. There is no guarantee of happiness, even for those who put in the effort. The Earth is slippery. It will move underneath you, they said, and swallow you up all the same. In a written conversation from the Mesoamerican time, a mother says to her child: 'The Earth is not a good place. It is not a place of joy, a place of contentment. It is rather said that it is a place of joy-fatigue, of joy-pain.'

To the people of that time, there was no distinction between those who made the right choices and those who made the wrong ones. It's a rudimentary analysis, and it is fair to say Toby has had years now to make a decision about whether to keep hurting himself and his family or at least attempt to get help. But, like the Aztecs would say, the Earth slipped beneath him well before now and he is, to some extent, at the mercy of two generations of family trauma reaching across time to him. Sometimes, the millions of tiny little moments of suffering take you down, like swarming ants on the carapace of a beetle. Nature.

Two days after the stabbing, Scott checked himself out of hospital and came back to our house. The patient band was still on his wrist and the left side of his face, with its injured nerves, had been hit by gravity. The doctors couldn't tell him whether the damage was permanent or not. Scott said there was some pressure in a blood vessel leading to the brain, but he'd left hospital because he was bored and it cost $20 he didn't have to hire a TV to watch. He didn't have a phone either. Scott was worried, too, about a new woman on his radar who, in his words, wanted to jump his bones, but he didn't know how he was supposed to go down on her now.

Scott was a career criminal, a petty thief. He would never leave our home town and therefore would consistently be caught by the police for his crimes. The first person to ever rob my family was Scott, who sent another boy through a window one day while we were at school to steal Toby's PlayStation games from his room.

When he came by after leaving hospital, he told me: 'At one stage I had about $82 000 worth of fines.' He was referring to court-ordered payments as a result of his offending. 'Don't believe anyone,' he laughed. 'Crime doesn't pay.' Then, without being prompted, he told me he'd run into his dad at the supermarket that same day. 'It was really weird, you know. I just didn't know what to say to him,' he said. 'He just asked me how I was going. I've never really had much to do with him, like Toby and his dad.' He paused, mulling over the quantum of his own feelings. 'And we live in the same fucking town,' he said.

When I first read *My Brother Jack* in high school, I only wanted to be a journalist. But so much about the lives of David Meredith and his older brother Jack mirrored my own. Raised by a loving mother and a less-than-perfect father, Jack in his blokey way won the backing of the family patriarch while David was considered with suspicion for his interest in books and writing. Their lives, in terms of fortune, reverse over time and Davy comes to be admired by Jack where it once was the other way around. I'm not sure if my brother has ever looked up to me or found me alien, the way I find him, but the book spoke a language I knew intimately: of David's sense of being a foreigner in his own family.

In the novel, David is told: 'You have neither the desire for this, nor the credentials with which to accomplish it. In a way, David, you are like some queer, strange savage who has journeyed a long way from his own tangled wilderness, and you look down on the palisades of the little settlement, and you wonder how you will pillage it and what trophies you will find.'

There was guilt when I first read those words—more so now—as I saw myself in that passage. I've trained myself to study my brother and try to understand his situation but I wonder whether I ought to feel more grief. There is an ache of sadness not just for him but for the thousands of others like him. If you could draw a line to the lives affected by a single drug addict you would eventually net most of the country.

Shortly before the saga spun out of control, a strange young man said hello to my mum in her yard at night. She couldn't identify his outline in the shadows.

'Hello Mrs Morton,' he said. 'It's me, Marcus.'

A decade had passed and Marcus, the snow-haired son of one of my brother's old girlfriends, was nineteen now. He'd moved to Victoria as a teenager but had then returned to our town and started hanging out with my brother again, this time as a young man. Mum pointed under the house and he went inside.

The lost boys smoked, together again.

CHAPTER 7

SINGAPORE SLING

It is rare for a person to become interested in politics until it personally affects them. Which is how, at the age of eleven, I became intensely concerned with the waterfront dispute that had floored the nation. The battle between the stevedoring Patrick Corporation and the Maritime Union of Australia, which ground on for months, was over worker rights and business productivity. But it came to visit me, all the same, because it made the VHS copy of *The Lost World: Jurassic Park* I'd ordered very late.

Chris Corrigan had formed Patrick Corporation with a mate, and it was his attempt to sack the unionised workforce in April 1998 by sending guards with Alsatians onto the wharves that triggered the war and the delay in my receiving the noted Hollywood sequel. Less than a decade later I would end up living at university with Corrigan's son, Joe, and realise I was still very mad about the whole ordeal. Soon enough, though, my friendship with Joe would leave me on the precipice of losing my first job as a journalist on account of an international dash to attend a hanging.

Some people go to the tennis, if the mood takes them, while worse people might turn up at the polo, an event for which there is no known purpose. The worst people, however, will pop up at another country's capital punishment extravaganza and take notes.

Joe Corrigan was weird. When I met him, his father had recently bought Virgin Blue (as it was then called) from Richard Branson and Joe's long-time fascination with aviation had reached fever pitch. He had rescued two sets of Qantas business-class seats and placed them in our living room. The electronics worked—you could recline fully, pull up the monitor from the armrest and watch television on it. He insisted we eat dinner on our tray tables, using crockery and cutlery he'd taken from various first-class lounges around the world.

Every day was like taking a business-class flight, which might have been OK if we'd actually gone somewhere. We never did, of course. Joe would just watch me and our other flatmate—his girl-friend—intensely while we ate to make sure we were appropriately enthusiastic about the seats. In my more desperate moments I could see him kidnapping some tourists and forcing them to cross-check and arm doors. The whole point of business class, I figured, was to re-create the experience of your living room while flying through the air. Attempting to re-create the re-creation of the experience of your living room while in your actual living room, on the ground, just seemed cruel. It was like going to Las Vegas to see the Eiffel Tower or giving your daughter an otter on stilts when she asked for a pony.

Things escalated when Joe decided to build a replica of a 747 cockpit in our spare room using actual aircraft parts he'd scavenged from mates at airlines. He installed a battery of computer monitors in the room, blackened by dark curtains, and ran his flight simulator on them. Then he flew to Malaysia. And he made me watch. This was shortly before news emerged of the Austrian man Josef Fritzl, he who kept his daughter locked in a basement for twenty-four years. Had I already heard of that case, I might have been more inclined to knock louder for my other flatmate to come and rescue me. I never did and, some eight hours later, we landed in Kuala Lumpur to cheers from Joe.

It was 2005 and we were studying at Bond University. Joe became my Rich Kid guide to this daunting private institution, where I was on a half-scholarship, with the rest of my $70 000 degree on student loans. His father was worth $200 million, while my family's most treasured item was a chook statue bought at a market. His dad was a businessman; we hoped to win the lotto. His family lived in a $6 million home in Sydney; we had a snake living in the wall of our rundown Queenslander that we couldn't get out.

During a valedictory speech at the university, the son of a Gold Coast property developer warned that Bond risked losing its 'elite status' because it was letting too many scholarship kids in. This struck me as odd because his family had gone bankrupt more than twice which, in itself, is a kind of scholarship. This was a place where money mattered more than grades and, unfortunately, I had neither of them.

It is often said of the Gold Coast that it is a sunny place for shady people, perhaps never more evident than in the founding of Bond University itself by the dodgy businessman Alan Bond. Everything about the university was designed to be 'exclusive', right down to the Masonic symbols hidden across the campus. The centrepiece is a water feature that runs down the central courtyard and under a sandstone arch. When viewed from above, the whole thing is in the shape of the seeing-eye pyramid that adorns American dollar notes and lubricates a litany of conspiracy theories. There are thirty-three uneven stairs running alongside this feature, one for each degree of Freemasonry.

The students were typically sons and daughters in Australia's richest families and, more impressive, in some of the world's most monied dynasties. Foreign princes and Bollywood stars came to study, as did the heiress to a Greek shipping fortune—a friend of mine—and sporting royalty. Students were bought Audis and Porsches on graduation by their parents.

Even though I had a cadetship—one semester of full-time work, one semester of study, with three casual shifts at the *Gold Coast Bulletin*—I never had any money, so I survived by doing essays and assignments for the kids who had money, which was everyone else. I stopped doing my own so I could focus on 'work', as it became. Word spread.

On one occasion I was sent by the newspaper to Brisbane to do a story on some large cracks that had appeared in the Riverside Expressway, shutting the biggest thoroughfare in the city. I was standing underneath the hulking mass of concrete when my phone rang. It was an American student who had been handed my number by a friend of a friend of a friend. He needed a law assignment done. My going rate was $500. Across three years, I wrote mostly law assignments. Promissory estoppel, torts, evidentiary law, almost an entire degree really. One of my regular clients is now a high-profile criminal lawyer.

Sometimes, the work got too much. I said no to an acquaintance of mine when she was in desperate need of an overnight turnaround on a 1500-word assignment. She begged me and asked me to name my price, which I was incapable of doing because every number seemed absurd to me. She named it herself, then withdrew $1500 and gave it to me. I did the assignment.

That I was poor was not new information, but after a lifetime of over-achieving at school I didn't go to two of my university subjects in my first semester. At all. I had the time but I no longer had the motivation. University felt like one more obstacle keeping me from the life I wanted. It wasn't quite so simple, however. The terms of my scholarship, and by extension my job, required I maintain a 75 per cent average.

Spending time with Joe probably didn't help my perspective. He had seen the world, flown on the Concorde jet (before the French ruined it for everyone) and had a credit card. I had been to the Gold Coast four times in my life before starting uni and my cadetship at the *Gold Coast Bulletin*. On all four occasions I went to Pacific Fair, then billed as the largest outdoor shopping centre in the world. It is not a very fun place, though I once thought it was. On one assignment I had to chase the wife of Shane Warne—they had just separated—through the maze of shops. It felt like a metaphor.

During my first-ever excursion to Sydney, on a road trip with Joe, he told me Bondi was mostly farmland and that the wealthy people kept their horses there. This made perfect sense to me, given it was a beachside suburb in one of the most expensive cities in the world. *Of course* the rich people would use it for agistment. I was eighteen.

We arrived late at the Corrigan family home, a sprawling period building in the Sydney eastern suburb of Woollahra, where Joe had to himself an entire mini-house at the back which adjoined the garage and his father's collection of Ducati motorcycles. One of the bikes was worth more than the entire amount Mum loaned from the bank to buy our first home.

We heard one of the motorcycles roar in late and Chris Corrigan popped his head in. There he was, the man who'd made my video copy of *The Lost World* late. He looked a bit like an Oxford law professor and almost entirely like a man who took joy in keeping my dinosaur movie out of the country.

'Dad, this is my friend Rick. How was your day?' Joe asked him.

'Terrible. Toll are going to launch a hostile takeover and there's not much we can do about it,' Mr Corrigan said.

I was not a business journalist. I did not know who Toll was. A hostile takeover, while it certainly sounded bad, also seemed like it could be used to describe a battle for bathroom resources among siblings. Just hours earlier I had readily believed the entire suburb of Bondi was a paddock, so I was in no position to begin analysing the significance of Mr Corrigan's weary phrasing. Nevertheless, Joe turned to me when his father had gone and commanded me: 'You cannot write about any of this.' Well, no. I didn't know what any of it meant.

The university's head of journalism, Mark Pearson, called me that same weekend. My results had come in for my first semester. I had notched an 11 per cent in one subject and, impressively, precisely zero per cent in another. 'What happened?' he asked me, the fury curdling at the back of his mouth. I searched for the right words, beyond the right words that were: Your course sucks and I'd much rather be at work.

I was four front pages into my fledgling career when I started the journalism 101 subject at Bond, which proceeded to teach us how to quote somebody correctly. It felt like a waste. Still, the program had a three-strikes policy and I'd registered my first by going AWOL for my debut semester. I chose to remedy this later in the year, not through any particular application of effort on my part, but by fleeing the country, going missing from work for two days and turning up on CNN at the execution of convicted Australian drug smuggler Van Tuong Nguyen in Singapore.

After almost two years of court hearings and appeals, Australian-Vietnamese resident Van Nguyen was sentenced to hang in Singapore on 2 December 2005 for the crime of arriving in the country with 300 grams of heroin strapped to his chest. When he'd been arrested in March the previous year, I was in my final run of high school and writing daily affirmations in a lined exercise book. 'I will be a journalist by the time I am twenty-one,' I wrote, at least twenty times a day. I don't think Van Nguyen ever thought to do affirmations. A man smuggling drugs into another country has given up on hope. What might he have written down? 'I will not be a drug smuggler in a country with capital punishment,' perhaps? Or 'I will find another way through the barriers of having been born in a refugee camp to get educated and make money, another way to pay off my twin brother's debt'?

Two days before the scheduled hanging at the notorious Changi Prison, around midnight, Joe called me. 'I'm going to go and see the hanging,' he said. This is not a thing people say outside of art gallery situations. Or maybe they did. I was beginning to discover the world was a much bigger place than I had given it credit for.

I was taken aback but quickly jumped into reporter mode: 'Oh, well make sure you ask some questions. Like, should the Singapore Government worry about its relationship with Australia after ignoring our pleas for clemency? How will this stop the illegal drug trade in the region?'

Joe was taking some journalism subjects, which is how we met, but he was a much better photographer. 'Come with me,' he said. That evening I had eaten pasta with plain beef mince and tomato sauce for dinner, again. I took home about $450 a week as a cadet. I had zero savings and no credit card. I could no more fly to Singapore for a death jaunt than I could make a functioning sweater out of bees.

'I'll pay for everything but you need to tell me because I'm booking it right now,' Joe said.

I was rostered on to work the next three days. I told him to book the flights and I'd speak to my editor in the morning.

Bob Gordon, editor-in-chief of the *Gold Coast Bulletin*, looked suspiciously like a lumberjack and had one of those editor's beer guts that could balance peace in the Middle East. His brother, an obstetrician in Ipswich, delivered my brother, sister and I over the course of a decade. Bob's specialty, on the other hand, was to rule with the kind of idiosyncratic fear-mongering beloved of tyrants, toddlers and religious scholars.

He frequently forgot the names of staff and, when pressed, resorted to calling them 'Tiger'. To reward good work he would place random items in a box and let reporters whose stories had, in his estimation, been the best yarns of the week rummage around for a prize. On one occasion a court reporter managed to pull from the box a metal wall bracket for a television. There was not even the pretence that she could choose again; it was simply accepted that she had been awarded a chunk of metal for her efforts. None of us were even sure if it was meant to be in the prize box to begin with but, like soldiers, we could never, and would not dare, question the process. I had never been honoured with a call-up to the prize box, but Bob liked me nonetheless.

There is a school of body language which holds that men who sit with their arms crossed in their laps are insecure. They are worried something is coming for their dick, so they protect it. This is all supposed to be unconscious, by the way. I'm not suggesting they are prone to installing Crimsafe doors and a panic room. It's just a thing. Editors, on the other hand, never do this. They are almost universally men and they appear to have been bred from the same hive editor. They sit with their legs spread wide, inviting you to come and destroy their junk but knowing full well you wouldn't. This is how Bob was sitting in his glass-walled office, all power and confidence, when I went to see him.

When I said I could cover Van Nguyen's hanging, Bob's response was: 'I'd like to reward your initiative.' Then he said: 'I need to think about it.' Then he never got back to me. The flight left the next morning with me on it, after I'd called the paper to say I was sick and couldn't come to work for a few days.

Singapore, a wealthy city-state under a so-called benevolent dictatorship, is very hot and very small. So small, in fact, that it has become the world's largest importer of sand. Its land size is 22 per cent bigger today than in the 1950s, when few knew or cared about it. The nation used to get most of its sand from Malaysia but this was not enough. By some measures, to reclaim 1 square kilometre of ocean, 31 million cubic metres of sand are needed. So Singapore turned to Indonesia for some legal sand imports. But it also straight up stole from its neighbour, in the process helping to wipe off the map at least twenty-four islands. The temptation was that, being an archipelago of some 17 000 islands, Indonesia had a lot of sand and fewer eyes watching it than almost anywhere else in the region. That the sand was necessarily attached to islands seemed not to matter.

It's not surprising, I guess, that nations steal things from each other. Intelligence, weapons, colonies. North Korea tried to burrow into South Korea to take back Koreans it felt belonged there, but they were sprung and tried to pretend it was a coal mine by painting the rocks black. To steal whole islands, though, grain by grain, is on another level, I find. It reveals a breathtaking commitment to the project beyond mere overtures. If you've ever built a retaining wall with a semi-capitalist autocracy on top of it, you'd understand.

But while Singapore actively smuggled hundreds of millions of cubic metres of sand into the country in the decades after achieving independence in 1965, its tolerance for drugs was less flexible. Indeed, its tolerance to anything outside the official order was low.

'Singapore is what your city could become if everyone obeyed the rules, did their jobs diligently, and just shut up,' author Jessica Zafra writes in *Twisted Travels*. 'When your city gets to be this paragon of efficiency and discipline, would you still want to live there? Singapore is a model city, which is terrific if you happen to be a model human.'

Australian and British prisoners were held by the Japanese in an army barracks near Changi Prison during World War II, while the complex itself was used to hold some 3000 civilians. It looked no less formidable when we asked the cab driver to take us past its walls after landing in Singapore. I don't know what I was expecting though. Gargoyles? Atmosphere? A featureless fence ringed the compound and international protestors were already camped outside, holding their vigil ahead of the hanging. Few locals were there. Dissent is not something that comes easily to Singaporeans and many, nonetheless, agreed with the verdict. Our cab driver did.

Nobody was present when Van Tuong Nguyen was hanged. His mother prayed in a chapel up the road. Not even she, had she wanted to, could witness the event. The convicted drug smuggler died alone at 6.07 on Friday morning, 2 December 2005. Afterwards, when Van Nguyen's lawyer, Julian McMahon, held a press conference outside the prison walls, the world's media hemmed him in. CNN, BBC, *The New York Times*, every television station and newspaper from Australia. The only press packs I have seen since that rivalled it for size were the ones that assembled for royal visits. I crawled beneath the legs of a cameraman and held my dictaphone up to the lawyer.

It is fair to say I had not thought through the logistics of my trip. Having called in sick to even be there, I now had a yarn I wanted my editor to run back home. It would require the spilling of secrets and an introduction to the thorny world of hostage negotiations.

The *Gold Coast Bulletin* did not have foreign correspondents. It had a Brisbane-based reporter and this was considered exotic enough. The two cities had little time for each other. Brisbane residents would duck to the Gold Coast for a swim, perhaps, but Gold Coasters almost never went to Brisbane unless it was for a flight to Bali or to attend court. And while the *Bulletin* might have been the largest regional daily newspaper in Australia, it saw no general benefit, even in the final golden years of print journalism, from sending a reporter to cover a major story whose victim was neither from the Gold Coast nor, dare I say it, particularly 'Australian'.

Schapelle Corby, who'd been arrested in Bali a few months earlier, was another matter of course. She was white, a beach native and had boobs, even if, during her trial, she often forgot things. She was perfect for the media. Corby smuggled 4.3 kilograms of marijuana in a boogie board bag, for crying out loud. The only way her story could have been more Australian was if she'd taken out a mining lease in the Pilbara while still in jail.

None of this mattered to me. I'd been there, I'd sat through the haunting silence at 6.07 a.m., I knew the Van Nguyen story was front-page news, and I wanted to write it. So I chose to blow my cover. Not in a particularly brave way, I should add. I knew I was about to unleash hell upon myself. So, sitting in my hotel room, I emailed the editorial secretary, Chris, a short note: 'Hi Chris. I know I said I was off sick but I'm actually in Singapore. I've got a story about the hanging. Can you let me know who I should email it to?'

Few things move faster in the universe than my chief-of-staff did that day. Light, certainly. NASA's Voyager spacecraft, perhaps. Karl Condon started his career in Brisbane and then he moved to the Northern Territory, which tells you almost everything you need to know about the man. A deputy chief-of-staff once fell on a staircase at a work Christmas party and bled all over it. Drunk himself, Karl called a photographer instead of an ambulance.

Karl was a man who moved on instinct and so it was, here. My phone rang. It was him. 'Rick, where the fuck are you?' he thundered.

This was one of those rhetorical questions. What Karl was really saying was: 'Rick, I know you are in Singapore and I am going to gut you like a water buffalo.' It was the kind of rhetorical question mobsters use for a flourish. A meaner version of the rhetorical question you ask a dog as you inquire as to its good boy status.

'I'm in Singapore.'

Answering such a question makes the questioner very angry indeed. Because they knew the answer and this robs them of the time to swear. As it happened, Karl used so many expletives that the only words left in his sentences were conjunctions.

Then he continued: 'You don't represent us, you're not to go down there, you do not work for the *Gold Coast Bulletin*, do you hear me?'

I mean, I did. But sure.

'You are coming back on the next flight.'

Complicating factor: the next day, Joe had booked us to fly the very short distance from Singapore to Kuala Lumpur in Malaysia. First class. After a night there, we would fly back Sunday evening.

So I told a white lie.

'Sunday, the next available flight is Sunday.'

'Good,' he said. 'Don't come into work for a week. We'll talk after that.'

Now, at this point I should have gone for a graceful commando roll out of the conversation. I had fled my home country on sick leave and turned up at an international execution. No need to complicate matters further, a reasonable person might say. But I was not a reasonable person. I was an idiot.

'Karl, can I ... still come to the Christmas party?'

The paper's party was due to be held in the week I'd just been told not to show my face. I'd never had a work Christmas party before. Certainly not one on the Gold Coast with a massive bar tab. Crisis aside, I had to know I could go.

Karl was thrown by the childlike innocence with which I had asked the question.

'The Christmas party? Well, yes. Fine, you can go to the party.'

Having set up a lavish defeat, you take the dirtiest of victories where you find them.

Informants back home in the office later told me Karl's face had turned a shade of hateful beetroot. He'd scoured CNN and other cable news networks to try to find me in the vision that played on a loop, as if seeing me there in addition to speaking with me on the phone might make matters worse. Karl was pulled into a news conference and never saw me.

I never filed a single word of the story to the paper, instead writing a piece for the university's own terrible press. And I was so afraid of having broken the rules that I kept my name off the story. My camera was broken and the only photos were on Joe's, which I never got from him. Except for the occasional slice of international news footage, there is no trace of my presence in Singapore. It was as if I'd never gone.

Joe had heard the whole conversation. With my boss off the phone, my world fell apart. I was going to lose my job. I was in a strange country, completely dependent on my friend for financial security. The cigarettes tasted funny—they didn't sell Longbeach menthols, favoured smoke of the teenaged girl from Townsville, in Singapore. I was inconsolable and Joe knew it after repeated attempts to engage me in conversation. He offered comfort the only way he knew how.

'Do you want me to get you a hooker?' Joe appeared to be joking. His sense of humour was warped.

Having legitimately fucked myself, I did not see how I could also fuck my way out of this. My family used to slaughter cattle for a living; I was not alive to the intricate politics of the workplace. My means of sorting this out were limited, to be sure, but engaging a sex worker was not one of them. Two fucks don't equal a right.

'I just want to get drunk, Joe,' I said.

So we did. My financier got us to meet up with a bunch of Qantas pilot mates of his who all had standing access to what was then called the Equinox Bar on the seventy-first floor of a tower in Singapore. The big-name Aussie TV journos were there and the city was laid out below us like a carpet of burning embers. You could see Indonesia. You could see its sand.

None of it seemed appropriate. A man had died that morning who should not have. And I was ordering double-shot rum and Cokes on an airline tab at an exclusive bar in one of the wealthiest per-capita nations on the planet. It was only when we stumbled into the Chijmes district and ordered mojitos and Joe vomited on the carpet of a hotel that I felt better.

I went on to discover there is not much to do in Malaysia for one day and a night. We bought lots of cheap DVDs. Joe rearranged the arrow pointing to Mecca in our hotel room. I insisted on seeing the Petronas Towers. Our cab driver honked at everything, including chickens. The chickens continued being chickens. Finally, what I had managed to forget regarding my impending doom was brought back on my return.

Those of us who worked for the *Gold Coast Bulletin*, and who had never worked anywhere else, believed it to be the centre of the world. The city had five theme parks, so the odds seemed good enough. We had undergone no Copernican revolution in regards to the newspaper's status. Real estate listings made it obscenely profitable. Just a few weeks after my jaunt, the paper would snatch the record for the biggest book size (page count) of any in the history of Australia. More than 600 pages. Most of it was real estate, which was cleaved off at the newsagent into a second section because the whole thing was too thick.

The paper took at least two cadets each year on the Bond scholarship program and had done since 1994. By the time I started, there were more than twenty-six current and former cadets somewhere out there in the wilderness or in more senior positions at the paper. The unbroken line of cadets came with its own mythology, none more harrowing than the story of Damian. He was just like us and then, one day, for unspecified reasons, he fucked up his time at the paper so royally that he lost his job and was flung out into the nevernever. We were told he ended up going to work in Toowoomba.

Toowoomba, for those unfamiliar with it, is a city on top of the Great Dividing Range known for its flower festival and a mayor who tried to ban porn. My brother and I almost killed a girl in Toowoomba. We were riding in one of those driver-equipped trains you find in the park, the ones with normal rubber wheels, and my brother started holding on to the carriage and running alongside it. I tried it, too, but found it harder to keep up, so I jumped back into the carriage. Then a little girl tried it because she had seen us do it. She must have been all of five and her legs had a difficult time keeping up with the speed of the train. To be clear, the train was going no more than 10 kilometres an hour, but her legs were little Jenga towers. They buckled and she was dragged under the wheels.

Her body created something of a Mexican wave under the carriages as they gently rolled over the top of her, and my brother and I had scarcely ridden the crest of what we presumed by then to be her corpse before taking off across the park, her cries piercing the summer air. I didn't sleep for weeks.

To this end, the tale of Damian the Exile in Toowoomba was as close to a believable ghost story as I was going to get. This was the salutary lesson invoked by the paper's chief police reporter, Tony Wilson, on my return to Australia: I was on my way to becoming a Damian, he warned, and it was not advisable that I attend the work Christmas party lest I cement the case. Tony was the unofficial mentor of all cadets. We called him the Lion King because he wore a mullet like a normal person wears a shawl. He also had a gold ring with the head of a lion on his left hand. We listened to him.

In lieu of the party, I went to Tony's place for dinner with him and his wife. We drank too much red wine. At midnight, all of us stumbling, Tony gave me a Cabcharge and put me in a taxi to get home. I bid him good night and promptly told the driver to take me to Surfers Paradise where the office Christmas party was kicking into high gear. The chief reporter, Peter Gleeson, was one of the first to see me. He threw his arms open and simply yelled: 'Singapore!' The features editor drummed up a nickname—I was his Singapore Sling, named after the cocktail invented at the Raffles Hotel and which, to this day, I have never tried. I was a hero.

The only two people who were angry about my sojourn weren't at the party. But I was pineappled by them all the same the following week. Pineappling is a blessed Queensland tradition that involves the bodily application of the rough end of the fruit. I don't know what it feels like to survive, say, Ebola but I feel like I can relate on some level. I kept my job though. Damian was banished to Toowoomba; I could stay.

But if second chances are a window through which you can glimpse your own failures, I was facing the wrong direction. The jump into my new life was so sudden and so fractured it was never going to end particularly well. I did not belong in this new world, though I had become distant from the old one. The old one represented everything I'd ever wanted to disappear from. The claustrophobia of it all had been rendered neatly by these new experiences.

When I was on the phone to Mum once, a friend's mother was visiting with me from Brisbane. She was a barrister and drove a convertible and wore jewellery that would have paid off Mum's mortgage. My friend's mum motioned to me to hand the phone over and she said to mine: 'Don't you worry about him Deb, we're taking very good care of him.' When I got the phone back, Mum seemed hurt.

'Do they know you already have a mother?' she said.

She felt the shame of not having enough money to take 'care' of me and I felt the guilt of the wonder I had incubated about this strange new place.

CHAPTER 8

THE GAME IS TO HIDE

In my last year of high school, the town we called home was forced to petition for broadband internet. Residents could have it, they were told, if they proved they would use it, and so for months we were asked to sign paper rolls that would demonstrate our intent to sign up with Telstra. This act of administrative enthusiasm got in the way of my being gay.

Throughout my adolescence, the only window to the gay world was through dial-up internet, though connecting to it stole the telephone line and made a noise so alarming it might have stood in for one of those 'scared straight' programs I'd read about. I didn't know any gay people. My friends didn't know any gay people. There was one character on TV who was gay. Well, I suppose his boyfriend was, too, but he didn't seem very happy with it.

We knew *of* one gay kid, an older boy who had moved to Brisbane and 'become' gay after high school. He was spoken of only in hushed tones, as if he had gone to prison or died at war. 'Did you hear Paul is *gay* now?' my friends and I would murmur. Paul had always been gay, of course, but we didn't know that. As near as we could make out, Paul had moved to Brisbane and been involved in a radioactive incident at The Wickham.

When I became that man, the one who suddenly 'turned' gay after moving away and moving back, a helpful resident of Boonah popped a message in my mailbox. It was a fairly meandering morality exercise that ended in the word 'faggot' and a half-decent picture of Jesus Christ on the crucifix. It did not escape my attention, almost a decade later, in 2017, that while getting ready to vote in a petition for my right to marry another man, I was receiving junk mail calling people like me an abomination.

Officially, there are more than 46 000 same-sex couples in Australia. There are many more people who are transgender or identify as queer, gender fluid or bisexual. Maybe one in ten Australians fall on this spectrum. Might be more, could be less. Who's counting? I never wanted to be among them and, in some small way, I never felt like I was. How could a man who won't accept himself ever feel included?

Long before I knew what the words meant, my father called every other person he didn't like a faggot or a poofter. He had elaborate ways of figuring out how to spot them, which mostly relied on the presence of a single earring in a man's ear. Paul Reiffel the cricketer was a faggot, Dad told me once when I was five. So was Shane Warne at one stage and some actor on *E Street*, which was a show I understood less than the word faggot. Mum was nicer, though her world experience was scarcely any broader. She had met a gay man once while working in her youth at David Jones in Brisbane. He had an interest in teapots, she recalled, which became both her red flag and her yardstick for measuring future gays.

Statistically, in those early years on the cattle station, it ought to have been possible that I had met a gay or lesbian person. But if

10 per cent of people are gay, then that presented problems, for it was only my father, mother and older brother Toby who lived permanently on the property. By my reckoning that means 0.4 of one of us was into the same sex.

Mum must have known, though even she mistook her early awareness for causality when I finally came out to her, aged twenty-one. The very first words out of her mouth gave it away: 'Oh darling. Was it the Ken doll I gave you when you were six?' I had already drunk 2 litres of cask wine on a friend's hotel balcony when I made the phone call. The box of Stanley was nestled on my lap as we spoke and I fiddled with the nozzle to top my glass up.

In late primary school, Mum would nudge me in the ribs when *Priscilla, Queen of the Desert* came on the television. I would pretend to be mildly interested while, in my head, planning how I, too, could be draped in 30 metres of space-silver fabric in the middle of the outback.

In high school I conducted a morning audit of the way I moved. I wanted rigid, manly gestures. My gestures had to be mountains, not flowing streams. I practised in front of a mirror. I kept a mental list of the names of girls at school who could be considered attractive so that I could name them should other boys begin the inevitable discussion. I never stared in the change rooms after sport. I found other cover, too.

The telephone company had just introduced a rather compli-cated feature, three-way calling, which was so new that nobody (me) thought to be wary of it. All I knew was that the thought of being on the phone to one person was tiring enough but three just seemed incalculably obscene. Anyway, the first three-way telephone conversation I ever had was also my last in a personal capacity. It was also how I got my first real girlfriend, which is a shame.

For reasons not entirely clear, a girl in my Year 10 class, Britteny, had become interested in me, and an eager mutual friend, Danielle, decided to do something about it. Danielle phoned me and began asking a series of questions about Britteny. 'Do you like her then?' Well, of course, I answered. To my mind the answer was given in the same way I might talk about my fondness for Ace of Base or chicken and mayo sandwiches but it certainly didn't mean I wanted to fuck them. By the time we'd made it to the end of the conversation I was a piece of sandstone worn down by the geological force of teenage sexual intrigue. 'So would you go out with her?' Cornered, and believing it was just myself and Danielle on the line, I said yes. There was a muffled voice on the line. It was Britteny. Danielle announced her to me as my new girlfriend in the style of a gameshow host revealing the grand prize is a new car to a contestant who was born and lives underground. My intricate game of pretend was made entirely more complex.

A week into my new relationship and Danielle was sent to me at the end of one lunch break, an emissary with a message to bear. I wasn't holding Britteny's hand during the breaks and had hugged her only once. This ought to have been a sign but it was construed as playing hard to get. Any confrontation with a teenaged girl could be considered an armed hold-up and so, at gunpoint, I began holding Britteny's hand. This sealed the early fissures in what she thought was a relationship and what I knew to be an elaborate ruse. I was torn entirely between wanting to preserve our friendship and wanting to appear straight, a survival instinct so strong I was living in unbearable stress.

The second big test of this messy dance came when my girlfriend invited me around to her house one Saturday afternoon. 'My parents won't be home,' she said, unzipping a duffel bag filled with hints and scattering them before me. Sometimes, when my brother and I were left home alone, we soaked tampons in petrol and used them as fuses to blow up cans of deodorant. Call it intuition but I suspected that was not what Britteny had in mind.

Her parents owned one of those L-shaped sets of square couches, from which we were to watch a movie. I waited for Britteny to sit on one far end before employing my scant knowledge of mathematics, following the imaginary hypotenuse between the two end points and sitting as far away from her as I possibly could. A glacier of awkward sexual tension, Britteny bum-shuffled closer throughout the movie until she had me pinned against an armrest with no escape route. There were explosions on the screen and, in them, I saw the inevitable destruction of my deceit. We never kissed.

I did all of these things because I was terrified of who I was and how people would react to me. From the age of twelve, I spent every day in witness protection. Every waking hour spent with another person was a gamble.

For his controversial essay 'The Epidemic of Gay Loneliness', the writer Michael Hobbes interviewed researchers in an attempt to understand the mental health impacts of being gay. It comes down not just to discrimination but the *expectation* of it. 'John Pachankis, a stress researcher at Yale, says the real damage gets done in the five or so years between realising your sexuality and starting to tell other people,' Hobbes writes. 'Even relatively small stressors in this period have an outsized effect—not because they're directly traumatic, but because we start to expect them.'

Travis Salway, a researcher at the BC Centre for Disease Control in Vancouver, says: 'No one has to call you queer for you to adjust your behaviour to avoid being called that.'

A study out of the Center for Mind and Brain at the University of California found that growing up gay is a lot like growing up poor. Too bad if you did both. The research revealed there were lower levels of the hormone cortisol among gay adults than the average. Cortisol regulates stress. In other words, gay people have their stress response triggered so often and almost without pause during their youth that the mechanism just stops working efficiently.

The stress comes not from being called a faggot every day or avoiding a hate crime. That might happen; it has happened to all of us many times. The point is that it *could* happen on any day and our mid-evolution brains activate the fight-or-flight response in advance. Think about when something in your home intermittently gives you a static shock. If it happens often enough in a short space of time, you become hesitant when approaching metal surfaces. You change the way you reach for the metal surfaces. Remember the rats? Now imagine the thing is not a static shock but something that goes to the core of your being. Endure that over and over again and by the time a person reaches adulthood, the damage is written into their bones.

These key studies were done in major cities of the world. I'm not sure they had ever heard of Boonah. It's not an especially terrifying place but it is relatively isolated from the rest of the world. It took three years after I moved away to find the courage to come out, but even then it was because I feared what the rumours would say back home.

I didn't belong in my country home town and I didn't belong in my city, having just come out as gay, either. The barbs of my life undercover were still in my skin. I didn't feel happy to be gay; I felt trapped. Whatever life I might have embraced as a proud gay man in the city seemed impossible to square with my internal hatred. I passed in both worlds, but neither of them felt like home. There is something to be said for this listlessness that is hard to understand if one has never been on the outside of anything. Many, though not all, gay people find their home in the queer scene. Perhaps it was my conditioning from a young age, my nature or both, but the 'scene' made me uncomfortable. Everyone was so confident—it was like they'd had two decades to ferret around in their psyches and come up with a way to exist vigorously. It was never that simple but that's how it appeared to this young man, fresh off the drying rack.

Coming out averted an imminent disaster but it wasn't going to hold me together in the long term. It seems hard to believe, even as somebody who has lived it, that these apparently small things can have such a sweeping presence in the lives of Australians in the twenty-first century. As Hobbes says in his piece, 'We bring the closets with us into adulthood.'

I was in Year 5 when Tasmania cut homosexual crimes from its criminal code. I was thirty when same-sex marriage was legalised. If that feels like a burden, what must the lives of those who went before feel like?

Michael Rogers was seventy-four when he first came out as a gay man. He was living at a Brotherhood of St Laurence aged-care home in Melbourne when something finally broke and he told a support worker. 'I have become a real person for the first time in my life,' he tells me when I speak with him. 'It was like living the life of a spy. I feel sad that I was unable to feel sad, that I was unable to admit or accept who I was.'

He's describing this idea that to get away with the cover-up, one has to dull one's senses and emotions. There can be no room for introspection. The search for a place to fit in even led Michael close to marriage with a woman. 'I was a confused person … I knew that it was men I wanted to be with but something inside me said "Oh you should be married, you should be with a woman",' he says. 'I became a Catholic and I was a thoroughly unbendable menace of a person. It was probably internal confusion. I was seeking some system that would say that I was right in my feelings.'

Michael, like all of us, was a product of his time. He came out as gay more than five years after I did but also five decades later, in real terms.

To this day, I have never had a relationship with another man. I'd like to, but I don't know how. Most of my twenties zipped by with me having no gay friends at all, something about which I was quite happy. When I first met Shannon, one of my closest friends now, I was afraid he would hate me. So afraid I downed two bottles of sauvignon blanc in quick succession and vomited it all back up while we were sitting smoking on a friend's verandah in Brisbane. 'There, there, get it all out,' he soothed, scruffing my hair in the process.

There is something insidious at work here. Gay people, particularly men, are modelled on an existence that expects rejection. They factor it in at every turn. Some overcompensate with these loud couldn't-care-less attitudes, others just go along with it like I do. The problem is that expectation informs reality. I didn't just *think* Shannon was going to hate me, I knew it. I have run away from or actively sabotaged at least three potential relationships because I was convinced the men were playing some kind of sick game where they pretended to be interested.

This fear is primed, at first, by family. Mum accepted who I was almost immediately. She had her own questions, as I did, but she loved me and she made it clear nothing would change that. I never told my father but would come to learn of his reaction nonetheless.

Sometime in 2014 my brother met with Dad for the last time face-to-face and Rodney told him up-front that he 'didn't like' what I was doing with my 'lifestyle'. That's it. There wasn't some great cataclysm. We hadn't even spoken for six years before that point. We had dogs that I knew better and had spent more time with than my father. Nevertheless, the man who had abandoned our family once was leaving me again, this time through words. That was the moment I finally became unseated from a throne of precarious ease with myself.

In a qualitative study of gay and lesbian Australians, the effect of family rejection is measured by their own words. 'You think parents have unconditional love and to, like, find out that, you know, how do I put it … that love comes with an actual condition. That was probably the hardest thing,' a woman called Emily told the study authors. 'Cause you like [starts to cry], I don't know, you expect things from people, you don't expect that from your parents.'

The authors go on to add: 'The fact that someone can reject a family member after coming out indicated a strong message that the gay/lesbian family member was generally unlovable. Facing family rejection for being gay or lesbian is not simply unacceptance of a voluntary and changeable aspect of an individual; rather, it is a rejection of a core component of a person—a central and unchangeable part of who someone is.'

What struck me reading the responses from young people in this study was how they directly and eerily mirrored my own experience.

A man called Tony told the researchers: 'I had always experienced anxiety and I could cope with it, but what sent me to the doctor was the fact that when this happened I couldn't cope anymore. This was what pushed me over. So other people that are in this situation, if they're already at a high level of anxiety and something like this is going to happen to them [and] it's going to push them over again, I would hate to think what avenues they might take in that situation.'

I had what I now know to be my first anxiety attack when I was twenty-one. Freshly removed from the closet, I was attending the first of my high-school friends' twenty-first birthday parties in Boonah. I hadn't seen any of them in person since the news broke that I was gay. I coped with the violent shaking and cold sweats by drinking myself into a stupor. For the rest of my twenties I kept these attacks mostly in check. They never became severe. Until the day I learned what Dad thought of me.

I now measure my life in two halves: the moment before I heard that news and the almost four years since. Happiness, always so difficult to pin down, seems more distant still.

In his 1989 *New Republic* essay which kickstarted the American debate on gay marriage, Andrew Sullivan makes a conservative case for access to the institution and recognises a fundamental shift in the way queer people interact with society at large. 'Much of the gay leadership clings to notions of gay life as essentially outsider, anti-bourgeois, radical. Marriage, for them, is co-optation into straight society. For the Stonewall generation, it is hard to see how this vision of conflict will ever fundamentally change,' he writes. 'But for many other gays—my guess, a majority—while they don't deny the importance of rebellion 20 years ago and are grateful for what was done, there's now the sense of a new opportunity. A need to rebel has quietly ceded to a desire to belong. To be gay and to be bourgeois no longer seems such an absurd proposition.'

Today in Australia there are some who still reject the notion of joining the team that never picked them. For the most part, however, we are sick of being on the outside. In the internecine, fifteen-year-long public battle for marriage equality, tempers have frayed and I've found myself caught in something of a Venn diagram of not-being-with-everyone-else. A gay man behind enemy lines, so to speak.

In 2014, while still relatively junior at *The Australian*, I was tasked by my editor-in-chief to write a piece about a gay advocate who had appeared on the ABC's *Q&A* program and whom the editor-in-chief believed was a hypocrite for having unsafe sex and talking about the HIV epidemic. But my chief-of-staff refused to ask me to write the story and, having heard about the editor-in-chief's request, I was incensed. The national broadsheet is a broad church but there was no way I would allow my sexuality to be used as cover for a hit-job news story that had no public interest value. When my higher-ups leapfrogged my chief-of-staff and demanded I write the story, I walked out of the office and went home.

The story never ran. That was the last of it. There were no repercussions, no sanctions. Life moved on. But it was this same activist who would later come to attack me and other gay staff members at *The Australian* for being 'complicit' in what he said was an agenda of hate against the queer community. He and others came to the conclusion that we were siding with the enemy by working for the newspaper and demanded we prove what difference we had made by being on the inside. He didn't know about that near-miss.

My mental health had never sunk so low. I felt I was being attacked from all sides for either being me or not being me enough. I was abused on social media by those who are disgusted by homosexuality and targeted by those who thought I was working hand-in-glove with an editorial stance that gave succour to the same anti-queer forces in our community.

For the first time in my life I was earning good money doing a job I loved. It was enough that I could help support myself and my mum and sister when times got tough, as they frequently did. I knew the effect our coverage had on young queer kids. I'd been there myself. But I also knew that leaving wouldn't make it any better. And doing so would cut myself and my family off at the knees after a lifetime spent trying to stand. These are the shades of grey in a person's life that always become collateral damage in a culture war. As the last year of my twenties closed out it became entirely clear that I had made little personal progress. I had left the country, where I never felt at home, for a city in which my sheltered upbringing was all too obvious. I was gay, though neither fully embraced by gay culture nor willing to fully embrace it. I was successful but still judged by parts of society as being unequal. Had devotion to my family immobilised my principles or was I just a coward after all? Culturally, I was a drifter, looking for a place to set down my things but never quite receiving permission, let alone a welcome.

Anyone looking for a reason to explain the rates of suicide and self-harm among queer Australians need only look at the shrapnel wounds of disgust and rejection they've collected over a lifetime. The rates are even worse in regional Australia.

One of the biggest longitudinal studies in Australian history, run by the Australian Institute of Family Studies, looked at more than 3300 teenagers who had suicidal ideation and who cut, burned or otherwise harmed themselves in the twelve months before they were interviewed at age fourteen or fifteen. Crucially, the researchers controlled for a litany of factors that might have made them want to do that. They looked at socioeconomic status, family structure or breakdown, individual characteristics and relationships. After doing so, only a handful of factors remained significant. The standout risk factor was having a sexuality other than heterosexual.

That's a big deal. Nothing predicts the deterioration of your mental health more than being queer. In the *American Journal of Public Health* we start to find out why this might be and it's not, as some would like you to believe, because being gay is a mental illness in and of itself. A study reported in the journal found that 'LGB respondents reported higher rates of perceived discrimination than heterosexuals in every category related to discrimination.'

There is much to treasure about being gay. It has opened in me a font of compassion that I'm not sure would otherwise have been there. It has played a role in formulating my ambition to succeed, which has driven me out of my poor teenage-year prospects and beyond the statistics. I hustled because I knew I couldn't stay in the town that had raised me. I worked harder because, well, what else was there to do? Maybe it saved me. Who can say?

Everything has a cost, however, and I've overspent. Those early years spent agonising over whether I would be found out and hung, drawn and quartered in the schoolyard have cast a lasting shadow. When everyone else was figuring out how to love and be loved, going on dates and breaking hearts, or having their own mashed into the soft earth, I was stuck on this quixotic project of self-preservation. My time would come, I reasoned, because it did for the others I knew. When I turned twenty-one I still told myself my time would come. Again, when I turned twenty-five. My fears burrowed deeper and deeper over time. The anxieties enmeshed with my vital organs. My heart became a tool for the expression only of panic. My time would come, I said yet again. Perhaps when I turned twenty-eight. I spent that year rushing between doctors and psychologists and slowly losing my mind. But the time would come, I said, once this was dealt with. Turning twenty-nine marked a return to the same episodic madness, and thirty represented an uneasy truce. The jangles are still behind my flesh somewhere, vibrating every so often with the accumulated dirt of two decades' reckoning.

As a nation, we have convinced ourselves that all of us has the same standing start, but this is neither true for the working-class whites from broken families nor for those with black or brown skin. It's not true for those without a proper education nor for those who were abused. Researchers call it 'minority stress', of which being queer is just one form. But it is one of the only forms where you go through it alone until the secret breaks open inside of you like a seed. You shoulder it on your own, keep your own counsel, make catastrophes of your own many futures. When the time is right you share it around. If you are lucky, the embrace comes swiftly.

If not, the bad counsel one kept is made incarnate by the reality of those rejections.

When I was in high school I used to spend my weekends and evenings rushing to hit 'record' on my tape player when a favourite song came on the radio. The dial-up internet made it difficult to download music; you really had to commit to a tune, which seemed an effort. My friends would make these mixtapes for their girlfriends or boyfriends, expressions of childhood love. They got to hand theirs out, secure in the knowledge they gained only via osmosis that this was what teenagers did.

I made them for myself, entire cassettes of the world's worst pop music. When no-one was looking, I danced.

CHAPTER 9

IN SEARCH OF SENSELESSNESS

I had three problems in 2015. One, I was not dead. Two, they had come for my blood. Three, if I didn't give it to them they would lock me up. But I had a plan to escape. It was not a particularly thorough plan, as plans go, but it had the key ingredient of all good plots. It existed.

It is fair to say I had the coping mechanisms of a bird that has just flown in through a classroom window, and it is also true to say that this led me to taking more painkillers than is recommended on the back of the packet. It is correct to add: the pain persisted and I saw my doctor.

It is a cruel fact of the universe that a person who tries to kill themselves is then forced to navigate, for the tenth time in two months, the doctor's waiting room. It's as if they are trying to make sure you finish the job. I started playing games involving people in the waiting room. I had to guess what they were in for. Broken toe. Misplaced lung. Lost a game of Monopoly and they were feeling sad about it. Caught penis in a zipper. Fallen down a flight of stairs while reading Kafka. Stampede of ducks.

They could have done the same for me but mine was more cut and dry: I wanted to die. To be perfectly accurate, I just wanted to not live anymore. The whole dying bit seemed, and was, awfully complicated. Dorothy Parker was about right when she noted the logistical problems with killing yourself. Drugs, razors, nooses. None of it seemed appealing.

As a child I stood perfectly on a nail that had become upturned in a sandpit, of all places, and my friends heard about it for weeks. The optics of being impaled on a nail while attending a Catholic primary school are a bit off, though, and all the teachers told me to shut up about it because I was scaring the other kids and at least two of the younger ones thought I was Jesus. That is to say, pain management is not my forte. Which is all well and good until you want to end it all. In this state you are a fishmonger with no fish to mong. You are entirely ill-equipped for the job.

And what do you do in such a situation? Die peacefully in your sleep? I often told myself I wanted to go like my childhood puppy Ollie, fast and in the night. The story becomes complicated when you furnish it with the attendant details: she was gored by a team of wild pigs, had her guts ripped right out. But the first bit, I wanted the first bit. A quiet death. So I took a box of Panadol instead, which, though dangerous, is a bit like trying to cure existential shame with Tiny Teddies. It feels … insubstantial.

Doctors, as it happens, take this kind of thing very seriously indeed because they hate any initiative at all on the part of the suicidal. They flat out reject all terms of negotiation. So here I was, chastened and sad, sitting in the same waiting room where only months earlier I had performed the most queer routine of my life.

I had had to rate my despair on a Likert scale. How often did I feel hopeless? Ten. Despondent? Ten. Suicidal thoughts? I didn't want to seem overeager. Nine. The nurse paused her little pause and chuckled nervously. 'Oh, that's not good at all is it!' I gave her one of those looks that says with incontrovertible commitment: Are you fucking kidding me? It is unfair to expect the woman whose job it is to rate emotions on a ten-point scale to have, say, a broader emotional range than the one on her clipboard, but I've had Barbie dolls with more appropriate responses, and one of them didn't even have a head.

My doctor, in front of whom I was now sitting, was much more compassionate. Or she had studied the facial movements one normally associates with compassion but instead of turning up to the right class, she ended up in a viewing room watching faces get squashed in a hydraulic press. When I told her terrible things she bunched her face together, melodramatically furrowed her brows and squeezed her features inwards, as if she were Renée Zellweger and had just been told some horrible news. And it worked, because it would lure me in and then I'd listen to 45 per cent of the things she said. But this time I told her I took a box of painkillers in one go and she immediately disregarded her concern routine and demanded I go to the emergency room. Right then.

Nemesis.

Just a month before, for the first time in my life, I'd dragged myself to the ER around 10 p.m. It was March, the night of my twenty-eighth birthday, and I was having the peculiar twin sensations of a panic attack combined with excruciating stomach pains. The latter felt as though I was being stabbed in the stomach (I assume) and the former felt like it always did—as if I had swallowed a box of bees and inside that box of bees was a vibrating mobile phone that you couldn't answer, and bees and phone weren't buzzing in any sort of synchronicity. I probably should have called an ambulance but I could hobble and I lived a twenty-minute walk from the ER so I dragged myself out of bed and staggered there.

After sitting in agony for an hour, surrounded by people whose maladies did not require guessing—one was clutching what looked like a half-sawn thumb—I was given a small cup filled with some kind of liquid. I vomited everything in a bathroom and then a nurse told me someone would be with me shortly for some 'tests'. I knew what that meant.

My first attempt at running away from a medical establishment failed on account of the fact I just pretended to be asleep in the back seat of a car. I made the very junior mistake of thinking doctors and parents, like the T. rex in *Jurassic Park*, have a visual system based on movement. This is perfectly inaccurate. I was only six and I got the tetanus needle. Such is life.

I didn't get an opportunity to test my key findings from that experience until twenty-two years later when I was sitting in that ER. The test man was coming to jab me with things and take my bodily fluids, like a creepy bowerbird who missed the memo about the things he should be coveting. I knew I had to get out of there. So when the nursing staff turned their backs, I clutched my muddled insides and dragged myself to the door and out into the world. Despite nearly collapsing three times on the shuffle home, I made it back to bed and finally fell asleep. In the low standards of the 'escape from hospital' genre I considered the excursion a mighty success. And I was prepared to do it again.

A month later, I said as much to my grimacing doctor as she implored me to go to the emergency room.

'I won't be doing that,' I told her.

'I have two options. You go to emergency now or I have no choice but to section you, and I'd really rather not have to do the last one,' she said.

'Section' is one of those weird terms medical people use when they don't want to say 'put you away'. One doesn't section the dishes from a dishwasher but one can be sectioned.

My doctor was resolute. My friend Bridie was in the waiting room, waiting. So I told a little lie: 'OK. My friend is outside. I'll walk down with her when we're done here.'

'Great,' the doctor said. 'I'll just call them now to let them know you're on the way.' And she picked up the phone and alerted the troops. My GP had checkmated the absolute hell out of me.

'Good,' I said.

'Good,' she said.

'Excellent,' I said.

'I'm glad,' she said.

Super-thrilled.

This was some *Minority Report*–level intervention. She had my measure. But I still had no intention of going.

There are three things of which I am absolutely terrified: affection, any spider and blood tests. I've had encounters ranging on the severity scale from mild to 'huntsman gave birth to a thousand babies in my living room' with both of the first two subjects, but I have never, to my knowledge, had a blood test. Yet it is this that I fear the most. I'd had this discussion with my GP thrice before. She'd wanted to check my levels. I had only before heard this said by someone examining an oil dipstick under the hood of a car.

Levels? I said no, she said I should, I said no. 'If you find me unconscious in a park one day, then you can take my blood,' I said. 'If you can knock me out beforehand, you can take my blood.' She said this was not a 'serious' suggestion, which showed how little she understood the situation I was in. It was deadly serious.

Ordered to the ER, I was shaking. I went outside and lit a cigarette and relayed the conversation to Bridie. 'I'm not going,' I said to her. I was scared. Not just because the doctor had told me my kidneys could fail, even a day after the painkilling attempt, but because I believed she would eventually find out I had never gone to the ER and call some kind of mental SWAT team to my house. The Suicide Squad. I didn't know what they were called. Maybe it was just one guy called Bruce. Maybe it was a robot, which would be cool but unlikely—a Roomba with a cup of tea on it bashing down my door.

Bridie had the rage behind her eyes that you only see when someone is scared and in a corner. She didn't say a word, just ground her teeth, glared at me.

Don't move, I told myself. Her vision's based on movement. I knew Bridie was assessing her options. 'You can't make me go,' I said to her, breaking the silence.

And then I prayed, or did what would amount to praying, and begged for an intervention. Not a medical intervention but something to break this impasse. A tsunami, preferably, but I would settle for a Jehovah or street urchin. Bridie and I both needed a reset on this curious set of affairs, to step back and look at our situation objectively. Her, in desperate need of a way to support a friend who had run out of tether, and me, caught in a pincer manoeuvre between two very distinct threats of pain: the one that eats away at your soul and the other that arrives intravenously.

I sat on a stone bench. And then, a miracle in the form of a man who fell on me. We hadn't ventured further than the regulation 4-metre no-smoking zone from the medical centre when this gentleman had an epileptic fit and collapsed into my side. As he tipped onto the ground, suddenly, my life had a purpose. A brief, singular purpose. I had to save this man, with slim to no medical skills. I held out my cigarette before realising that this was not a scalpel or anything that someone would come and take from me while I saved a man's life, so I threw it down and got to work.

'Somebody get a doctor!'—screamed from the footpath by a woman who had clearly paid attention in drama school. The man was convulsing and I was, I don't know, sort of holding his shoulders and head because I had nine-tenths-of-zero knowledge about what to actually do. And then the doctor arrived. My doctor. The one who had banished me to the ER not fifteen minutes before. She gave me the kind of look that says, Did I literally not just tell you to go to the emergency room? It was a look I was beginning to notice popping up in my life with an unwelcome frequency. And then she attended to the man who was in more immediate danger, a kneeling metaphor for the health system at large.

In breaking open his own tongue with his teeth, this unheralded stranger had broken the ice. Bridie turned to me and said: 'What do you want to do?' I replied: 'I want a coffee.' So that is what we did. We had coffee. And made dark jokes about my dark life. We did it because, in truth, neither of us knew how to properly manage the contours of my depression, which at times seemed to be entirely without form and at other times would burst into relief, fully realised as a thing with sharp and dangerous borders, a thing with animus.

I still don't know what damage the pills did to me, but I got lucky, in a way, and lived. On the phone that night, having received no visit from the Roomba or Bruce, we joked again.

'And Bridie, this chapter will be called The Day We Saved a Man's Life and Almost Ended Rick's,' I told her.

'I'll save you just so I can kill you,' she said.

I had always been an anxious child and my seven-year battle with resentment while I was coming out, or more precisely, coming to terms with being gay, set in concrete a deficiency of personality. I thought, despite all evidence to the contrary, that everyone I met would be disgusted by me. The world's disgust and shame over me, cast from a mould used by my father, would be inalienable. It would be as pure and incorruptible as my sense of fear of the people around me. What had once sat dormant was building inside me.

Had I wondered what led to my breakdown, in retrospect I might have applied some sense of foreboding, some forewarning, and it might have been seen as dramatic embellishment. But my notebooks in the two years leading up to it were filled with such warnings.

In October 2014 I wrote, while apparently attempting to emulate the diary of a teenaged girl: 'I am trapped. I am so close to screaming. I fear a meltdown is just over the horizon. I'm standing in a railway tunnel and the wind is starting to push past me and I can hear the shriek of wheel on rail from somewhere *just* down the way. Do I lie down on the tracks and wait, or run? Neither seems to be a palatable option.' My body had been doing its version of the birds that take flight before an earthquake hits. The dogs were barking too.

When I was in high school my town experienced a spate of suicides. One intelligent girl I knew, who had suffered a brain injury after crashing from a motorbike, couldn't live any longer the way she was. She couldn't do maths, her forte. So she grabbed a rifle after her parents had gone to church one Saturday night and blew her brains out. Another young man, who served us weekly at the local supermarket, hanged himself in a garden shed. My friend Tara swallowed a bottle of pills one night and never woke up.

Much of what would send me spare in my twenties had already happened to me by then, but none of the damage had set. I could not contemplate then what it would take to remove yourself from the world, and it seemed as foreign to watch other people try, and succeed, as watching eukaryote cells fizz about under a microscope.

Suicide becomes an option somewhere along the way, when all other options cease to become viable. Or at least that's how I sold it to myself as my body broke into my mind.

It was the anxiety that did it, as cruel a force as was ever produced in nature. Depression had come and gone for years, nasty enough in the way a formless blob can be nasty, but it was, if anything, a morose sidekick. I'd come home some nights from work and it would be there, drinking whisky on my couch in its underpants. And I would tell it to move out and it would, after four months. Or I'd tell it to pay rent and it would, in some perverse sense, allow me to gain something from it. Something else formless, but a gain all the same.

The anxiety was not this fellow. It was a thing with a trillion spring-loaded points and when you get it in you, you don't get it out. Anxiety is a feeling in search of corroborating evidence. A sense in search of senselessness. And it finds what it wants, what it needs, every time.

Two months before I took the pills, the panic attacks were keeping me up most of the night. I was getting three hours sleep if I was lucky and then only because of exhaustion. The attacks were so strong my body continued them without my conscious self, waking me up so I could fret and agonise properly. I'd make lists of every person who'd said they loved me but who I knew for sure did not. I used my father as evidence, the Morton family yardstick, and I overlaid everyone else onto him. Then I made lists as long as the Magna Carta for each of them and became an expert in semiotics. An unanswered text was a glyph in want of meaning, so I gave it meaning. I poured explanations like concrete into long silences. I became convinced of my own powers of meaning-making. I analysed words and actions not as a scientist would, for they must report what the evidence tells them, but as a disbarred practitioner might reconstruct evidence to fit their prior understanding.

And my prior understanding was simple: that I was not loved. And the evidence rained down on me. It was truly a miracle.

I'd beg for morning so I could put on a face—stoic?—and turn up to work. As is the way of comedies, I suffered through this routine while acting-chief-of-staff, and while on a NSW election campaign bus in the north of the state. I also did it while on a twin-propeller aircraft that flew out of a Sydney 'storm of the century' to take me to the funeral of a school teacher who had been murdered. During the ascent the flight attendant chirped: 'I'll come around and give you drinks … If I can stand up!' Her laugh was kind of hollow, like a depressurised cabin, and I gripped the armrest.

There were moments, such as when the plane attempted to land in torrential rain in Orange, that even my frayed sense of self allowed the humour in. The Rex aircraft had almost hit the runway when the throttle was pulled and we shot upwards, away from the ground. Silence for twenty minutes, as we circled over regional NSW in the dark. Then the flight attendant came back. 'That wasn't on the itinerary,' she chuckled nervously. I screamed inside myself like I had with the nurse: *Are you fucking kidding me?*

But the universe had already announced its intentions, if the beginning of 2015 was anything to go by, and I was starring in a one-man stage play of little cosmic importance. I knew it, whatever was out there knew it, and we all of us found it absurd.

In the justice system, the poor are given court-appointed duty lawyers. I know this because I did work experience with one in Year 11 and also, not insignificantly, because my brother has used quite a few of them following his own personal pursuits. What one cannot know beforehand, really, is that a similar system exists for psychologists.

My Newtown psychologist, Marcia, was one of those perfectly affable professionals who manage the dual sensory inputs of both your own personal despair and an astonishing temporal awareness with remarkable ease. I first started seeing her in February 2015, as my descent quickened. Things were heading for a break-up, however, from the moment she handed me a manual the size of a small dog filled with activities. Here I was, straddling a neurotic fuckstorm, and she was giving me *coursework*. For every half-hour block I was awake, which in my then circumstance was about forty-two separate instances every day, I was required to write down what I was thinking about, what I was eating and what I was doing. Bizarrely, the boxes into which I was expected to inscribe these lengthy reports were about the size of a single Excel spreadsheet cell. In fact, I think this is what they were. Whoever had originally drawn this table could not or would not expand the size of the cells, marking the whole project for failure before one could even begin.

I tried to keep a more consistent diary once, when I was six. It was a little blue lock-up job with Aladdin on the cover and in it I wrote some of my most secret thoughts, such as my low opinion of cattle, what I thought were the directions to a cousin's house in suburban Brisbane (these bore no actual resemblance to real life), and a picture of my then governess (who would, in a few years, become my step-mum) holding a knife. Things were going swimmingly until my brother picked the lock with a paperclip, at once boosting my appreciation of magic and ruining the fledgling idea that my thoughts could be protected mechanically.

When I stopped keeping Marcia's diary, she sighed and asked why. I was frustrated. My mental health plan expired. The plans are granted in two blocks. First, six sessions are approved and then if you still need more—as if you wouldn't need more—you have to visit your GP again and have them extended by four sessions. And then, that's it until the new calendar year. In the midst of a crisis you can see a psychologist for an hour once a week, for ten weeks, and then … nothing. Marcia was free but the others I have seen all charged about $220 a session, or about $70 after the rebate. I earned good money but with no other support mechanisms the sessions came at a cost.

Renée Zellweger was away when I went to renew my plan late in 2015, so another GP's face was added to the pastiche of my unravelling. I walked gingerly into his office and told him I needed a new plan. And he did something that I was not expecting. He threw up his hands in exasperation and yelled: 'This is going to take fifteen minutes! I haven't had lunch and I've got other patients waiting!'

I protested, shocked and furious. And then he kicked me out, sans plan. A doctor.

My mother raised me not to be a hateful person but here are some things, in no particular order, that I wanted to happen to this man: Mishap with fire ants. Ennui. Premature ejaculation. I wanted him to experience the feeling you get just before you tip backwards off a chair, but I wanted him to feel it forever, like I was. But mostly, and I regret feeling this only partially, I wanted him to fall irretrievably down a well.

One suicide attempt is bad luck. Two, it may be said, is carelessness. Little more than a year later, in the 2016 Christmas dead zone, I found myself, drunk and through tears, navigating a series of Chinese-language websites trying to purchase Nembutal from an overseas supplier.

I'd read a feature article by one of my colleagues about online euthanasia communities where people swapped advice about how to buy this drug. It kills you quietly and within the hour. For those watching on, it is as if the person fades into a deep sleep. Then they stop breathing. All you had to do was get your hands on it, illegally, for about $500 a pop. The feature told the story of a young man who was not terminally ill but who wanted to die—my story, more or less—and how the members of the group he contacted shared their advice freely and without checking. So I followed in his footsteps and placed my order, then cried deep into the night, alone, in my inner-city Melbourne apartment.

In the months before, I had grown close to a straight man. Not romantically, as such, but in a way that meant I found his affection intoxicating. It was something I had been craving all my life but had never found. Not from my father, nor my brother. I had seen it in few men and, when I had, it scared me. You build the walls to keep it out, normally. You build them sturdy and towering, not because you fear what lies outside them but because you know what you'll do to it when it gets inside.

He was the third person I had let inside. The warmth of his demeanour, the free flow of his kind words, his masculinity. It all served to remind me not of my worth as an individual but of my father's inaccessibility, of his disdain for my character. And so, armed to the teeth with insecurities, I would test the boundaries. I knew that he could not love me in the way I needed and all I had to do was find the point beyond which even he was willing to go. It never takes particularly long.

I had forgotten about the death drug by the time it finally turned up in my letterbox. It felt like possibility in my hands. The simple act of having it in my house made me instantly feel better. It scared me, but not nearly as much as it energised me. It was money in the bank. You didn't have to spend it all at once. But you *could*. No more Panadol for me. I was on the *up*.

It came as a powder, surprisingly, and I transferred it to a small container I purchased from a chemist. Then I put it in my pantry, next to the spices, made myself salmon and couscous, and slept soundly for the first time in a month. I laughed darkly about mistaking it for cumin while cooking and thought *that would be hilarious*. Come for the cumin, gone for eternity.

Still, the powder scared me, and I told this friend what I had done. He was away for a week-and-a-half so it was a kind of insurance policy against misadventure while not being a particularly good one. What could be done to stop me from such a distance? It seemed like a decent concession to friendship. I had not been entirely scurrilous. My friend's advice over private messages was slanted towards what not to do: Throw it in the bin, no wait, someone might take it. Don't open it, you might breathe it in. Don't pour it down the sink, you might kill an ocean.

When I told my psychologist, he also thought I should get rid of the powder but seemed genuinely stumped on the method. 'Maybe pour it in the garden bed?' he suggested. Curiously comforting, I thought, that even the expert has been reduced to improvisation.

I have wanted to die more times than I can count because I have not yet found a way to be loved in a way I can trust. But just a few weeks after my thirtieth birthday I found myself lying in bed with a man who I knew loved me deeply as a friend and with whom I had occasionally shared a kiss while marinated in drugs at house parties. We were both in our underwear, legs wrapped around each other. It was an odd moment of solace. I traced my fingers through his chest hair and around the event horizon of his belly button. Around and around. My fingers combed through the trace of hair from the lip of his belly button to the top of the elastic band on his boxers. Occasionally, I rested my head on his bare chest and listened to the thump of his heartbeat. Like mine, it had quickened in the dark.

He had a girlfriend. He loved her. And yet through a mild drunken haze, he told me he loved me, too. That I was one of just three men he had ever been attracted to. He slid his hands along my face, feeling its outline like a blind person would.

Why, I asked.

He laughed gently next to me. It had not occurred to him that I genuinely could not place, in time or space, his reasons. And so, in the bed, he gave them to me, piece by piece, while my arms held his stomach and chest.

The moment was euphoric, for both of us, and devastating, for what it meant. It had dawned on me slowly that this particular kind of moment was one I had never shared with anybody. I had never had such a gentle passport to another person's body while they told me they loved me. I had never been so close, physically, with a person whose love I did not doubt. It was the absence of my own corrosive doubt that made that slice of time engorge itself. I had been alive thirty years and didn't know things like that could exist. That I could trust another man so resolutely and give myself over to the pleasure of being close to him. It felt like wearing glasses for the first time, for the heart. I didn't fear losing him.

Running away from the emergency ward, scrambling to dump a euthanasia drug sent from China in the post—it's all very dramatic. It is the plodding lethargy of every other day that does you in. There is a pause, sometime between the 42 453rd and 42 454th time you've attempted to explain anxiety to a friend and been rebuffed by their own inexperience, that you get a sense of the overwhelming isolation that has long awaited. Everyone who suffers mental illness has this moment, planted up ahead on the tracks like an improvised explosive. All one has to do is roll over it.

I have lived with severe mental health issues for more than three years now and the hardest part to deal with is the complete incomprehensibility of it all to those looking in. The medication I am on makes me feel as if I am drowning in molasses and yet I must still work. The anxiety attacks are invisible and yet I must still work. I have made my living describing things to other people and yet I cannot really explain what this all feels like to my closest friends. Nor even to another person with a similar illness. You could take 1000 accounts of anxiety and they would all be different, all triggered by entirely dissimilar things. If you are lucky, the combination of therapy and interventions and pills might stave off the worst of the symptoms. Maybe you will even get a doctor who does not kick you out of his office when you're trying to renew your mental health plan.

I have danced along a line, never entirely clear, between keeping my turmoil private and spilling it to people who have only ever been shackled to their own definitions of it. That is, I suppose, the fate of all human beings. We live alone and die alone. The interior remains a mystery, compounded under the creaking stress of insanity. I am unknowable to both myself and to you. I am unknowable to medical science. I have been, at my worst, unknowable to my own dog. And dogs know everything.

My medication has induced an exhaustion so cellular and integral in my body, that my bones are sleepy. The heart, pumping without intent. Above all, I have become tired of having to try so hard just to *be* in the world. To have the understanding of close friends, to experience their patience. To be a facsimile of a prior self. Legible, perhaps.

Of course, I am not alone, not really. There are millions of Australians who suffer from mental health problems and at least 290 000 require some form of community support in any given year—though the services available to them are sporadic and possibly designed by a Byzantine planner who was kicked out of the empire for being too complicated. And when things went pear-shaped in Melbourne and my little secret became less so, my boss

Gemma was an extraordinary saviour. There was no judgement, no questioning that moving me back to Sydney—which would cost the company thousands of dollars—was the right move to help. She made it happen immediately and it was all locked in. Gemma rescues cats in her spare time—she once found one at a press conference and adopted it out to the treasurer—so I shouldn't have been too surprised.

Still, I have lost count of how many times I've called a cab to take me home from the office in the middle of a panic attack. The sensation is so familiar now. Sitting in the passenger seat screaming internally while trying to hold together the outward appearance of normality. The landscape blurs around me, part rush of anxiety, part motion blur. The cab driver tries to speak to me and I try to respond but my sentences come out clipped and staccato, as if they've emerged from a malfunctioning production line at an engineering firm. Words clanking together, words that don't fit.

In October 2017, my prescription medication expired and I pottered off to a new GP in Redfern. Without pause he told me I had been on this dose for two years, then said: 'I'm going to bring you back to 50 milligrams. Just pretend you are still taking 100 milligrams and I'll see you in eight weeks.' I had been feeling good, well-put-together, and didn't think to question the sudden call. My GP did not discuss potential side effects with me. He didn't give me a contingency plan. Our appointment lasted all of four minutes, and most of that was the blood pressure test.

The human brain is a terrifying thing. Within a day my anxiety had ratcheted up to such a degree that I was having panic attacks at least once a day. I took four days out of five off work, turning up on a Wednesday just because I was acting chief-of-staff. I wanted to run away the entire day, sure that I was going to be fired for being so out of it. I took the panic as a temporary fluctuation while my brain readjusted. Within a week, however, the sense of total doom was pervasive. It was 2015 all over again.

I woke like clockwork around 1 a.m. and then 4 a.m. for four nights in a row, unable to get back to sleep properly. The fear produced by the anxiety itself was overwhelming but this time I also had the fear of how bad I knew it *would* get, based on my previous experience. Throughout the days, the terror was so intense and prolonged I wanted to scratch it out from under my skin. There was not an inch of reprieve. Little sleep, no rest during the day, constantly on the lookout for the ways in which I was hated and unloved. I soon found the evidence I needed to convince myself there was no rescuing friendships, no holding on to the last of the belief that I had any value. And still the jackhammering of the heart and the nerves. It was the staccato destruction of everything that had kept me functioning.

I booked an appointment with my GP with the sole intention of getting a mental health plan. And I searched desperately for a psychologist with an immediate opening. Dead end, dead end, dead end. Here's where luck comes into it. I messaged the fiancé of my close friend Shannon on Facebook. Rob runs two psychology practices in Sydney and I begged him to find me someone who could see me. He came back within half an hour with two options at his practice. What could I have done if I was still poor and had no contacts in the system? What possible solution might there have been?

That afternoon, a series of events merged together that pressed every single button that had ever formed my crushing condition. I caught the train home and power-walked to my front door and, once it had closed behind me, I howled. Sobbed so violently and consistently the glassware rattled on the sink. I banged my head against the wall to stop the jangling and ran a kitchen knife along my wrist, testing my capacity to deal harm. Couldn't do it. I settled on swallowing pills again, whatever I had in the house. But only if I couldn't raise my friends in a last-ditch attempt at self-preservation. Without informing Bridie of the extent of my troubles, I was turned away—pregnancy sickness and a full house. So I reached out once more, more brutally this time, to another. I said I wanted to kill myself and that I didn't know what else to do if I had to spend the night alone.

This is the zenith of despair, for what it is worth. The culmination of a week's lack of sleep and a lifetime's lack of love. This was it. If I didn't hear back, I was going to do my best to end it. But I did hear back, spent $100 on smokes and an Uber fare, and wept loudly for three hours on my friend's balcony. He cooked me dinner and slowly unpicked the tangle of my fright.

Here is a very interesting thing. The next morning I saw my GP again and he immediately bumped me back up to 100 milligrams of my medication a day. And the following morning I took my first restored dosage of the medication. I can pinpoint the precise stretch of road—Elizabeth Street, between McEvoy and Redfern streets—when the terror withdrew from the top of my head like a rocket ship. It happened in real time. The same thoughts that had so totally unbuckled my life were rendered anew. This time, they were just objects in my head. No threat level, no doom. Inanimate objects floating in my consciousness. In a matter of just minutes I had my old life back.

I don't understand it, the way the chemicals can do that to a person. I walked into the office. I told jokes. My eyes smiled.

Is it possible to be on the outside of the outside of the outside? Or perhaps that is the seventh circle of hell. Having grown up poor and gay in country Queensland, now with mental health problems. I'm not sure how that gets read out at bingo.

In a way, one can trace the seeds of my illness back to the 1920s when my grandfather was born, and to the 1960s when my father was brought into the world under the autocratic rule of his own. It's not that every gay man needs a father. It just helps when the ones you already have don't leave.

The first time I experienced complete mental despair and tried medication, it dulled the ferocity of my panic attacks. I woke up one morning in September 2015 after the first full night's rest I had had in half a year and I cried, because I was happy. I wrote an email to Bridie and another close friend, Seamus. Sometimes, when I read that email back, it makes a lot of sense. In other, darker, moments that have followed, I wonder how I could ever have felt like that. And that's the guts of it, this oscillating understanding of light and shade.

I choose to believe the words written in the light of my own happiness are the least distorted.

CHAPTER 10

OUTSIDE IN

My first cadetship in newspaper journalism ended as improbably as it had begun. I had just turned twenty-one and I was having a shouting match with the editor of a community newspaper on the Gold Coast when I told him to get out of his chair.

This wasn't the first stage of an invitation for a physical fight, though I'm not sure he knew that. Shane was a lean bloke from the bush and he'd been in a few bar fights in his time. I was a rotund and shy cadet with arms like pool noodles. Shane stood, and I sat down in his chair. I began to type my resignation letter. It was short and crisp and, like the best poetry, it told a story about the macro in the micro. The words 'effective immediately' were included in there somewhere. The whir of the LaserJet printer punctuated our awkward silence before it spat out the page. I signed my name and dated the letter and walked out of the offices without saying goodbye to anyone.

Three years, three months and I was finished.

I have always found the yellow smiling-sun-face buses on the Gold Coast to be among the saddest in the world but the journey back to my apartment in Surfers Paradise took on a peculiar and vivid anxiety. Queens of the Stone Age's 'No One Knows' crackled through my second-hand, second-generation metallic-pink iPod. I went home to an empty apartment I shared with my Greek shipping company heiress friend, took the rest of her cocaine and vacuumed the carpet.

Though I cut my own rope on the executioner's platform, the conditions under which I was led there were expansive and thick, a kind of molasses for the soul. My friend and workmate Monica had known the end was near and wrote me a poem. I remember it all because I thought it so profound I almost had it tattooed on my shoulder.

I wish I was that cockroach, set free from the Sun, off to merry insect hell on a flea-ridden coach.

When I was growing up, the pointy-headed doom and gloom of current affairs was not for our family and I had almost zero exposure to it. Mum's life was hard and we relaxed by watching soap operas, reality television and *The Today Show*. I can't remember a time when we had ABC-anything on, let alone the radio. It sounded boring and stuffy and all the famous people were on the commercial TV stations. We loved famous people.

On a rare trip to Brisbane Airport to see off a friend, Mum stumbled across the Parramatta Eels NRL team. She couldn't resist and heckled them.

'The Broncos are gonna smash you tonight,' she said in gentle tones.

The captain's reply was excruciating. 'The game was last night. And we flogged 'em!'

In my shame I managed to snap a picture on my cheap film camera. It was blurry and overexposed but I succeeded in selling it to a classmate in high school for ten bucks.

Mum was interested in politics in the way most people are: superficially. She saw the top stories on the commercial television news and lent her vote in elections according to the candidates who bothered turning up at her door. May the good Lord help anyone who left a leaflet in the mailbox without popping in to say hello. That was a sign of someone who thought they were too good for us. 'Oh him, he thinks he's God's gift to man,' Mum would often say.

There was no time for the complex analysis of deliberately opaque government policy because Deborah Morton was a single mum with three children and a job and several chickens, two dogs, two cats and a cockatiel called Cisco. If Bruce Paige on Channel Nine couldn't get the point across, we just went on living.

I wanted to get into journalism for two reasons, neither of them fully informed. I could write because I could read and it seemed a fine job for writing. And it was a job that paid. We had no reference point for what a well-paying job was but something inside me said journalism was a profession for the rich and well-oiled because I saw a TV reporter get out of a helicopter once. On all counts, I was horribly misled.

The first time I was published was in Year 7 after our end-of-year inter-school camp in the mountain ranges around Boonah. I wanted to thank the teachers for organising the event—it had long seemed obvious to me that children were hell—and I wrote a letter to the *Fassifern Guardian*, the family-owned local newspaper. Seeing my name in print was electric. I don't imagine I thought it at the time but it seemed to lend my very existence a credibility it had lacked. Newspapers, though I scarcely understood them, were the places where history met its first draft. To be a part of that, even in the service of thanking the local teachers, elevated my life above the grind. What does anybody look forward to when they are young? Some cranial niggle told me the usual aspirations would not be for me. No early marriage, no children to bear the best and worst parts of me out into the world and beyond my own existence, no grandchildren. I had no plan for my life beyond leaving some kind of mark, preferably one left in ink and checked by a subeditor.

The media isn't filled by people from 'state school, battler backgrounds', as a friend of mine at the ABC told me once. Where diversity quotas exist, they tend to be by race and culture or even sexuality. This is a fine goal but even these diverse hires come from remarkably similar nooks by way of class. The ones who make it into the media typically come from comfortable families in comfortable suburbs. If they haven't attended a nice independent or private school, they've attended a good state school. They have choice. If their spirited attempt at jagging a gig in an industry known for crushing the hopes of thousands fails, they have backup options. Crucially, they have a family with the resources to support dead-end careers.

By this reckoning, I ought to have done law like I'd intended. I had the marks, it would definitely pay and I could probably do it. If I failed at journalism there was nobody to catch me.

It never used to be that way, of course. Newspaper journalism was a respectable trade in the last century. Anybody who thought to enter it could be nurtured by those who went before them and guaranteed a proper wage or salary and the kind of career progression the legal fraternity enjoys. It was messy, dirty and required only vast reserves of pluck. Everything else just fell into place. Kids from working-class backgrounds became cadets and rose to become editors because Australia was small and inward-looking. These rough and ready types could talk to anyone, most often in a bar, and had the easy swagger of the man and woman with nothing to lose. You know that confidence when you see it; it is draped in the scars of a million tiny battles.

Everybody knows the story about how newspapers (and other media more generally) forgot to be worried about the internet and ended up haemorrhaging cash. It's one of the greater miscalculations in history short of several wars and the entirety of my high school maths effort. The financial pain didn't just hurt the work of the free press but also fundamentally changed the entry system.

In his 2009 report on universities in the United Kingdom, former cabinet minister Alan Milburn, together with twenty experts from across academia and industry, finally revealed the worst-kept secret in media. Journalism had become one of 'the most exclusive middle-class professions of the 21st century'. The report is, bleakly, filled with headline news. Of those born between 1958 and 1970, it says, the biggest decline in social mobility has happened in the journalism and accounting professions: 'Journalists and broadcasters born in 1958 typically grew up in families with an income of around 5.5% above that of the average family. But this rose to 42.4% for the generation of journalists and broadcasters born in 1970.'

In 2002, a report from the UK's National Union of Journalists had produced data from the largest-ever survey of new entrants to journalism that showed that just 3 per cent of them grew up in homes headed by a semi-skilled or unskilled parent or parents.

This is a madness.

Early in my career I was trying to get my head around business journalism. Business seemed to me to be a sort of otherworld into which few were admitted. Like Heaven if you were a Catholic. I asked a colleague why she became a business writer and not, say, one who covered politics or social affairs. 'Everything comes back to money. It took me a while to see it at first but you soon get a feeling for the way business makes politics turn and vice versa,' she said. 'Follow the money, there's always a story.'

Following the money, like the arrow of time itself, is a one-way street. It means looking up, not down. Pick the thread and chase it to the top where the money accumulates. That's journalism, or so it goes.

I remember thinking: What about the people with no money? Who follows them? The answer today is fewer and fewer people. An industry charged with the powers of observation and record keeping ought to understand the people about whom it is asked to account.

Folker Hanusch built on some early studies of journalist demographics in the 1990s to chart the decline of the working-class scribe in Australia. Take 1992, the first year of his comparisons, when almost half of all journalists working in the nation had no formal education beyond high school. That figure dropped to one-third at the turn of the millennium and plunged to 12 per cent in 2013. In the same period, those with university degrees jumped from one-third to three-quarters of journalists. Read into it what you will, but the proportion of journalists who described their personal politics as 'left of centre' rose over the two decades from 39 per cent to 51 per cent.

When I went to university in 2005 I was the first of twenty-one cousins on my father's side to do so and the third of ten on my mother's side. As the nation moved towards a knowledge class, the Mortons doubled down in their suspicion of it. Like Tasmanian families, my Queensland and South Australian relatives knew that higher education took people away from the land. What the land needed was not a degree but sons and, in certain cases, daughters who were willing to stay behind and work it and breed. It was, and to an extent remains, a feudal system in its simplistic expectations.

When I first moved out of home, just shy of my eighteenth birthday, I was flung into a city that I had visited only a few times—the Gold Coast—ninety minutes east of my home town, enrolled in a university degree and employed as a cadet journalist. The rare fights between my mother and me took on a new dimension entirely. 'Ever since you moved out of home you think you're better than us,' she spat at me once when I was visiting. I can't remember what precipitated this, though I imagine I said something short that wounded her pride.

The hurt was as big as class itself. This idea that your own child can move beyond the contours of your life, that they might be embarrassed by you, that you did all you could and it may not have been enough. These are the fears of any parent but they are particularly the fears of a parent who has been subjected to the full impact of the worst kind of social mobility: moving backward.

The discomfort was as small as steak, too. On one occasion I went out to lunch with my mum and Lauryn and we ordered steak. Influenced by our time on the cattle station, we had only ever eaten our steak one way: burned beyond even the identification powers of forensic science. When I ordered mine medium rare, then, it came as something of a shock to my sister. She responded in humour, but it said so much: 'Oh, lah dee da rich boy.'

I turned eighteen having never tried any foreign food apart from the lemon chicken at my home-town Chinese restaurant. This isn't necessarily unique. Being worldly is not a defining trait of any class. But almost every person who lacks the means and the resources starts off in a shell, insulated against other people and cultures and ways of being in the world.

The reverse is true, of course. The middle class and the properly rich tend to move in their own herds, pay for their own schools, socialise with their own kind. The effect is not as severe, however, because they will always have the means to go beyond. The extra cognitive capacity that comes with not having to worry about money or even work is freeing in a way the worry of the poor is shackling.

When the time comes, this knowledge becomes a reminder you are acting out of your station.

When I was seventeen, I made the short list for the vice-chancellor's scholarship at Bond University. The package would pay entirely for any degree you chose to do, even two, and at Bond this could easily be worth more than $150000. The stakes were high and the hoops many. In the final stage they brought thirty-three would-be students together on campus where we lived for a week during our high school holidays. We were put through challenges, interviews, cocktail receptions and dinners to assess not just our academic abilities but whether we could hold our own as full citizens of the professional class.

I was hopelessly out of my depth and I didn't make the final eleven. Not because the selectors saw in me some classless bogan from the back blocks, but because that's how I saw myself. There is discomfort in being immersed in your own shortcomings. The kids who had come from well-off families, and almost all of them did, were at ease. They seemed to glide through the world on a cushion of their own confidence. They were almost without exception lovely, kind, smart and worthy people. But this world belonged to them and they knew it.

When scientists at the Large Hadron Collider underneath Europe discovered the famed but heretofore hidden Higgs Boson in 2012, it proved the existence of the Higgs Field, the pan-universal net made up of these particles. This field, invisible to all of us, is what gives particles their mass. Think of it as like trying to get to a famous person at a party. Everyone else is in the way and they create a sense of drag when you make a beeline for the person; they hold you back.

This is how I came to see the thousands of tiny, often individually low-impact markers of class in my own upbringing. Piled one on the other they created this net that had been thrown over me and people like me. We watched others with more 'civilised' families get around with smaller nets or no net at all, slipping through the ether with the aerodynamic ease of familiarity.

During the final dinner that week at the university, when we were still being watched and prodded like army recruits during a pre-deployment physical, all thirty-three of us went out to a teppanyaki restaurant. The chefs were throwing prawns and seafood at us and we had little bowls of rice, and for the first time in my life I encountered chopsticks. I watched as everyone wielded their little sticks with precision and I tried in vain to copy them. At the cocktail function later, I didn't have a suit. Nor, even, a pair of smart chinos. It must have looked as if I'd wandered into the wrong room while searching for the student assistance office. Later, I cried.

With the early death of a defined nobility, the tale of Australia as a meritocracy prospered. For the longest time, it was largely true. At the height of manufacturing in the 1960s when the sector represented one-quarter of the nation's GDP, blue-collar jobs in a growing nation grew faster than the suburbs. Professional jobs existed, of course, but in the same way that the town down the road existed. You could still get to it. The gap between the richest and the poorest was narrower and the economy rewarded those who did tangible things. And then this status quo flipped.

Though the build-up was long, the dramatic revision of work and effort was finally laid bare by recent crises. Australian National University historian Frank Bongiorno writes: 'The global financial crisis inflicted serious wounds on the meritocratic myth by vividly demonstrating that financial rewards have become radically disconnected from merit or usefulness.' According to Bongiorno, the GFC demolished the post-World War II 'social compact', and its re-establishment is not a given. 'The myth of meritocracy survived partly because it was still possible to argue that those who were sufficiently talented and industrious could make their way up the social ladder, despite their class disadvantage,' he writes.

Possible, of course, though harder than ever.

Then there are the culture warriors. They and I are interested in the constituency of journalists for different reasons. They assume more reporters are barking from the left because they are 'elite' and have never stepped outside their own bubble. This rankles because these same commentators have spent so long inside their own bubbles—many were even born in it—that they receive their mail there.

My colleague Peter van Onselen skewered this parasitism in deft fashion when writing in *The Australian*. 'Making matters worse, an entire industry has developed that thrives on this dysfunction, as well as criticisms about the club-like nature of politics. It whips up anger among listeners and viewers doing it tough. We hear it on the radio waves and see it on populist television programs,' he writes of the political class more broadly. 'Ironically, most of those who spruik criticisms of the "insiders" are themselves the ultimate personification of what the system churns out. I can't think of too many commentators who rail against "inner-city latte-sipping lefties" who get their coffee in the outer suburbs. Why would they, so far from their expensive homes in the inner suburbs? What these free speech warriors are really railing against is free expression they don't agree with, and they falsely subsume themselves as part of the masses to give their criticisms more weight.'

One type of assassin bug from Africa springs to mind. It literally stacks the corpses of ants on its body as a protective shield against predators. I'm not saying this is precisely what some in the commentariat are doing, but they might be enthused by the innovative approach.

We don't need more journalists from the right or from the left. It's the wrong approach entirely. What the media needs—what it should desire, actually—is more reporters with the ability to understand their subjects. There is a small problem with the repetition of our egalitarian myth and that is this: repeating it doesn't make it true. We never hear from the people for whom this myth failed and when we do, we feel instinctively that they are to blame.

I've heard friends in the industry say that higher power prices are the cost of fighting climate change, writing off the hundreds of thousands, if not millions, of Australians for whom the slightest bump in their electricity bill means a deeper slide into poverty. It seems silly to say it, but they're right. Most of the world's experts who have the benefit of having studied the matter agree. And yet, these offhand comments are callous because I am uncomfortably familiar with the pressure my own mother is under to pay her bills each month. That's not a pretend concern. In the crossfire, my mum's story is co-opted or dismissed by the ideologues and very often at the hands of people on either side who have never once lived a day the way she has lived her life.

Mum is open-minded towards climate change, without ever having the time to read extensively about it, but whatever concern she has about the future is mediated by her desire to survive the present. Neither extreme in the public debate understands her and, to be frank, it drives me wild. At a certain point, you need to be fed. Or your family needs to be fed. Is it any wonder, then, that so many people when presented with the opportunity of further study cannot afford to do it? This isn't about whether education is free or whether the student loans scheme is up to the task. They work well enough but they are only half the solution. We all get to try the option, this much is true, but we do not pay the same price.

There are those who would tend to view this as a sweeping political statement but they, too, would miss the point. When you're trying to survive you don't give a fuck about the culture wars. Nor, even, about identity politics, or being 'woke', which is one of those terms fashioned to suit a fashion. To be awake to problematic behaviour as defined through the prism of identity politics is noble enough, I suppose, but only some people have the time. What has become problematic now? Who cares, we're trying to put fuel in the car for night classes. Living, for so many people in Australia, is *exhausting*.

One of the major failings of progressive politics in Australia, indeed around the world, is a preoccupation with the grievances of the middle class. Put another way, this brand of politics prioritises the woe of people who can afford to worry about anything other than paying the bills and feeding themselves.

I was something of a dreamer as a child and, thankfully back then, these realities were yet to bite. Even so, particularly as a teenager, there were some things I knew. There was a sort of shadow in people wrought by poverty, a meridian running constant across the terrain of their own constitution. Some people made it out and up, but most did not. The income quintiles I read about in high school were like reserved seating at the cricket—the members' stand was for members only, and so on and so forth. What it took to get ahead was, I reasoned as a young man, luck. And if luck was all I had, then maybe writing my affirmations about becoming a journalist twenty times a day, all in identical sentences, wasn't such a dumb idea after all. Perhaps ambition, certainly the kind I had, is just a version of idiotic faith.

When I made my second application for a scholarship at Bond University, this one tied to a cadetship at the *Gold Coast Bulletin*, I assumed I would get the rest of the money I needed through government loans. At the time, in late 2004, the Higher Education Contribution Scheme didn't actually extend to Bond, but I distinctly remember being told after I won one of the two places in the scholarship program that a new loan scheme for private institutions would come into effect in 2005. That seems like a fun fact but had I started a year earlier I might never have made it as a journalist at all. I might have done the degree at a regular university only to run up against a wall of unaffordability elsewhere. The problem? Internships.

They are the perpetual motion machine of modern media. The traditional entree in relation to jobs has all but become extinct and uni grads are now required to enter the colosseum of work experience as unpaid interns. Winner takes the job in an industry that is collapsing.

In a moment of pique I questioned an industry colleague's promotion of seven-week unpaid internships at a large media company that rhymes with Schmairfax. The responses handily illustrated how feebly people from the middle classes, and beyond, understand the limitations of capital. 'Some people who deserve those opportunities can't afford to work for free,' I wrote. The immediate response, and I must stress that this is the very first thing I received from the colleague in reply, was this: 'For fuck's sake, Rick. Get over it.' Unfortunately, my class barrier doesn't come with a stepladder, or scissor lift, or whatever it is people use to be socially mobile these days.

Another person chimed in with: 'Getting into the industry I never got paid. I took it as an opportunity to learn and get a foot in the door.' When pushed on how he might have afforded this, he said:

'I worked weekends.' If you live with your parents in the city where the internships are held, sure, you might get by. You might even get to go out drinking with mates and enjoy being twenty-something. This bloke, or any of the dozens of others who wondered what all of the fuss was about, didn't come from a regional town with no public transport links to the cities. Maybe his parents could afford to support him around the edges.

The point isn't disdain. We'd all be there if we could. The ignorance chafes, however. There are those who have had the good fortune to never have felt anything other than the silkiness of privilege, their bubbles so perfect they cannot feel the gravel underneath. And that's what it is. Silkiness. When you've grown up in a vacuum, the very idea of friction seems alien. Yet that's an internship, just more and more friction. These unpaid, time-consuming exercises grant what students need most—experience—but they come at a cost.

The journalists' union in Australia helpfully explains that internships should not become a 'source of free labour' but in some companies this is precisely what has happened. Fairfax announced its round of weeks-long internships after a major tranche of redundancies. At News Corp, where I deputise as chief-of-staff, I've relied on a free body when resources get thin to handle a story from start to finish. I have always tried to sit with them at the end of the day and go through the copy, line by line, and answer any questions they have, but the reality is this is never as thorough as it might have been a decade ago. These interns, almost without exception, come from families whose resources have indirectly given them permission to fail.

Some media companies are selecting for urban and middle-class voices even when the gigs are paid. A friend of mine from a regional Queensland town made it to the final round of cadetship interviews at Fairfax Media in Sydney. He's a talented young guy with oodles of newspaper experience in local communities. More, it turned out, than any of the others who had applied. In the end, however, he was told point blank by one of the interviewers: 'You're a bit too much of a country bumpkin for the audience.'

This is a particularly Sydney problem, which makes it a some-what national problem. The great media houses and networks are all headquartered in Australia's largest city, where chatter about the kind of school a person went to is almost as common as the internecine debate about property prices.

When the *Guardian Australia* launched, my friend Bridie was one of the few reporters there who hadn't gone to a Sydney private school. That changed as they expanded, but it took years. Bridie and I started our cadetships together at the *Gold Coast Bulletin* and, as we both migrated south to the global city, we noticed there were fewer and fewer people like us. We bonded because we came from similar backgrounds, and even on the transient tourist strip that counts as a city north of the Tweed, we were the odd ones out.

There is probably no better example of how media works to reinforce those on the inside than the case of a former cadet at *The Australian* who was given a years-long crack at success in journalism because he happened to be the bloke who brought the former editor-in-chief's bins inside on rubbish day. His father, and by extension the would-be-journo, lived next door in an exclusive street, so the introductions were guaranteed. When his pestering finally paid off and the boss offered him a cadetship, his own father quietly asked the editor-in-chief: 'Are you sure you know what you're doing?' The cadet had a former life—in architecture—but his designs were on the masthead and his idea of the prestige it lent in the political circles within which he spent much of his time. The truth is, he wasn't much suited to journalism and now runs a bar. He spent years in that newsroom taking the place of someone who would have burned more fiercely for journalism.

When I started my first job as a cadet in 2005, I didn't have a car or a driver's licence. I cannot count the number of jobs I turned up to late because I was waiting for a cab on the road outside the giant blue shed we called an office in Molendinar. Karl, my chief-of-staff, told me very early on: 'Mate, if we have to keep sending you everywhere in cabs you're not going to get very far.' So I paid for myself to get driving lessons. About a year later my grandmother died and Mum received a small inheritance. She gave me $4000 to buy my first car, a little red 1990 Toyota Seca that came with a CD of African tribal music and a dodgy flange, which was a word that entered my life shortly after the vehicle did.

A cascading series of failures put me right back to square one when I ran up the arse end of another car while on my way to a story at work. I was young and naive and, thinking my insurance paid the towing fees, opted to have the car towed. I was illegally renting a friend's on-campus accommodation at university and left the key in the wreckage. When I went to get the key and my other belongings back, I found out the towing fees were more than $300 and I couldn't afford them. A day later, one of the university cleaners locked my room door while my friend was in Peru and I could no longer get inside. In the space of a few days I had lost my car—just six months after I'd bought it—and my home.

While I couldn't pay the towing fees, I could just afford to rent a dodgy Toyota Starlet from a Surfers Paradise company on a discounted rate, and I slept in that until my friend returned from overseas. I kept the hire car for eight months because I was terrified of the consequences for my cadetship if I was again without a car. I earned very little and was living ninety minutes from my home town with no financial support, so the $160-a-week rental was solely on me. I paid this and about $170 a week in rent, which ate up almost two-thirds of my take-home pay.

A year or so later another cadet offered to give me his car as long as I made the repayments to him. It was worth about $3000 and was a manual, which I didn't know how to drive, but I figured I would learn. An American university student borrowed the car just weeks after I took possession to take his girlfriend to the airport but it broke down on the side of the M1 near Beenleigh and he left it overnight. By the next day it had been torn to pieces for scrap by opportunists. The American never told me what happened and he only paid me $500 before he left the country. I paid the $3000 to my workmate as promised and spent the rest of my cadetship without a car. I never did get to drive this second car.

Constantly broke and worn down by the humiliations of my sexuality, I stopped going to university properly, began drinking heavily—over one two-week Christmas period I drank a bottle of rum a night while dancing alone in my sharehouse—and sabotaged my promising career in the most spectacular way. On some days I turned up to work still drunk, smelling of rum. More often I was hungover and scarcely capable of bashing out a few hundred words. I was told I would never work for that company again.

That I was trying to embark on a career as a reporter when I was least capable of doing it is not just my story. It belongs to a great many of us, some of whom you'll have never heard of because they went into other things. It's all very well and good. I'm not one of these types who thinks modern journalism is a heroic empire guarding society from the terror of the unexplained, though it can, at its best, be exactly that. Nor do I think journalists uniformly deserve to be exiled, by way of public ill favour, with the used-car salesmen and whoever it is that runs Danoz Direct. Granted, I have, on occasion, wished mild discomfort on different reporters at different times, but that just makes me normal, or an editor. The question I'm most interested in interrogating is this: Does anyone honestly believe the product would be better if we left its creation only to those well-oiled few who were able to have a crack?

You know where the class boundaries are kept when you find the people who aren't truly, truly running on empty just to stay still. The inability to recognise what it takes simply to get by while poor goes both ways.

Around the time the Coalition was considering introducing a $7 co-payment for anyone going to the GP on Medicare, I pointed out that this could be the difference between eating or not for a person on the poverty line. I was thinking of my own mother when I said it. She had recently got to the stage in her life where, after the bills were paid and the shopping done, she could save enough to buy one takeaway hot chocolate at her local cafe once a week with her friends from work. A libertarian fired back on social media, arguing that it was just a return bus fare and why couldn't people afford that. I politely explained my mum's situation. Incredulous, he said surely there must be something she could cut out. Smokes, alcohol?

'My mother doesn't drink, smoke or gamble. There is no wriggle room here,' I wrote back.

The man's response shocked me, though it ought not to have. 'I don't believe you,' he said.

Faced with the experience of people and a class he'd never belonged to, the man simply chose disbelief rather than admit that perhaps he was wrong about the ability of people to fish around in their wallet or purse for seven bucks.

When Tim Winton said there are those who see poverty and discern only a failure of character, he was talking about people like this. Libertarians, I have noticed, are the kind of people who deplore the government unless they're begging it for tax breaks. Everything else is a handout.

Class is access. To resources, to culture, to the conversations people are having *about* you. For the longest time, as a child, I had no idea the conversation about us and people like us was even out there. My ignorance was built on generations of accumulated concerns: survival, rent, food, repeat. No time to make the world big. No-one to make it big for you. That it happened to me is still a matter of confusion.

The gig that finally brought me to Sydney, the cocaine-addled heart of media in Australia, was as a news editor for the women's website Mamamia, which was founded and run by former magazine editor Mia Freedman. It was a blog written while I was bored and working for the Queensland Department of Education late in 2010 that snared their interest, but I, dear reader, was as surprised as you are that I ever ended up there. I went to Sydney to start in the Mamamia office in February 2011, not only moving cities and states but also going down an income tax bracket. The others who worked there, dear friends all, came from moderately wealthy and upper-class families. The bosses were staggeringly rich. It was impossible to find a reference point for that kind of wealth and equally my colleagues could not fathom the life I had led. There were frequent attempts at empathy but it sounded a lot like people who were reading pre-prepared lines. Imagine a fish turning up to discover her psychologist is a Very Concerned sea eagle.

The breaking point in a job that had otherwise devoured me came in April 2012 when two Indigenous teenagers were shot by police after they drove their stolen car onto the footpath in Kings Cross, mowing down pedestrians. They were fourteen and eighteen years old.

'It is unforgivable. They put people's lives in danger,' my boss ranted.

'You are discounting everything that has happened in their own lives to this point,' I screamed back. 'Do you honestly think they woke up this morning and thought it would be a good idea to run some people down on the footpath? Whatever happened today was put in play before they were even born.'

I was furious. Not because my boss had voiced concern about the (white) victims in the event, but because she had refused to consider any of the structural forces set in motion by their race and socioeconomic status. This was not because she was mean-spirited but because she had precisely no reference point in her own life.

I wanted out. Mia Freedman kind of wanted me out as well, though she was not about to fire me. Instead, I told her I wanted to leave. She asked me what I wanted to do. The answer: newspapers, again. I had had my time in the wilderness. Now I wanted back in.

Mia emailed the then editor-in-chief of *The Australian*, Chris Mitchell, whom she had never met, and told him about this young man in her employ: 'He has newspapers in his blood and I think you should have coffee with him.' It was the kind of bolshy move people with vast networks made; Mia wrote a Sunday column in the News Corp papers at the time. For reasons beyond my comprehension, Mitchell said yes.

Coffee turned into a three-panel interview with Mitchell, then-editor Clive Mathieson and *Weekend Australian* editor Michelle Gunn. I could see that the look on Clive's face during the interview process very much said, What the fuck is going on here? Years later Clive would tell me at a pub: 'You were the weirdest fucking hire we ever made.'

I began work in July in *The Australian*'s newsroom, the secret child of a Mitchell executive decision. Two months later more than twenty people were made redundant but I was given a full-time contract.

Four years after telling my then editor to get out of his chair and resigning, four years after abandoning my university degree and moving back home, destitute, I had made it back to my first true love.

Nobody knew who I was.

CHAPTER 11

ESCAPE VELOCITY

It ought to have been obvious by the middle of high school that the world was a place I would forever be required to solve or reckon with, always having to try just that little bit harder to make sense of it.

Mum had taken me to a shopping centre with a new cinema chain called Readings, so I could see a movie, but the name had thrown both of us into a manic spiral of confusion. Her theory, and increasingly mine as I adopted her concern, went like so: Was this entire chain a series of movie theatres with subtitles for the hearing-impaired? The problem was born in the hollow left by our innate sense that subtitles were for weird families and would ruin the cinematic experience, in this case a viewing of the noted classic *Scary Movie 2*. As neither of us could work out what the name meant, Mum asked the poor attendant.

'It says it's a Readings cinema. Is that with words?' she asked.

'Um, yeah, it has words,' the attendant said.

'So it has the words that come up under the pictures?'

There was a long and fertile silence, during which several acres of shame could be tilled somewhere in my body.

'It's just a normal cinema called Readings. That's the brand name,' the attendant said.

And there it was, the simplest of answers, which had never crossed our minds.

As it turned out, the cinema had a policy of not allowing those under fifteen to see MA15+ movies without an adult present, even if those adults had given their permission. Mum began an extended argument over her rights as a parent, which got us nowhere. We ended up going and eating a KFC lunch together instead, which is when part of the chain caught fire. 'Oh God Rick, they're going to think it was that crazy woman,' she said.

All our lives are like this, of course. We are filled with countless little moments that test the borders of our personal universe. Some of us are exposed to them gradually throughout the course of our childhood and adult years, while others are thrust into swarms of them in quick succession.

When it came to her kids, Mum was determined to show us as much as she could. Occasionally, her mother Mary would dip into her own savings to fund a school trip. Which is how, the year after the Readings incident, I ended up in Germany for a month with my language class. When finally shown to my room with my host family, I went in search of a plug with which I could charge my camera, though naturally none of them fitted my Australian appliance. This is effectively a horror movie to a fifteen-year-old nerd.

Several pre-planning evenings held by the teachers at my school had covered off almost every conceivable aspect of the trip and what we would need to do to prepare. But this—buying an adaptor—was considered so basic as to be assumed knowledge. Imagine my surprise when I learned that different continents used entirely distinct power points. It was like waking up to the realisation I had been living in a super-low-key version of *The Truman Show*.

A few years earlier my family accidentally stumbled onto the idea of vegetarianism in practice, at a barbecue hosted by one of the nurses who had treated my brother for weeks on the burns ward in Brisbane. If we'd had our way we might have learned about it under more comfortable circumstances—perhaps with easy access to a steak. I knew something was wrong when I saw the look of fear in Mum's eyes, the same look she used to get when we discovered snakes had died and decomposed in our rainwater tanks. Mum separated me from our hosts and shepherded me into a deserted hallway where she leaned in and whispered: 'They're vegetarians!'

It was the same tone my father would have used if he'd accidentally wandered into a gay bar. We'd never met any vegetarians before and we were scared. At the age of eight, I wasn't even entirely sure what one was.

'What does that mean,' I asked, conjuring images of a cult from which we would have trouble escaping.

'There's no meat! They don't eat meat!'

The idea that you could be invited to a barbecue without any kind of animal on it was anathema to my family. Springing vegetables-only on the guests was, to our minds, a betrayal. A barbecue that is lying about being a barbecue. You'd be better off covering yourself in lettuce and having a cry in the bath. Mum was surprised, I think, to see so many side dishes and only found out the truth when she innocently inquired: 'Where's the meat?'

Alive, apparently.

On the drive home Mum apologised profusely. 'They said it was a *barbecue* Rick, a barbecue! How was I supposed to know there wouldn't be any meat?'

Escaping your parental umwelt is like blasting into space aboard a sputtering rocket ship. It's an almighty task but one that renders any return trip in new light. You see your old habitat through the prism of everything else, out there. And it's oh so small.

Your parents prescribe a set of dimensions in which you are to live. They govern the most trivial things and are the foundation for the most meaningful. And one day your parents are gone, superseded by this strange new world in which they are fallible, utterly human creatures. You have seen how the magic trick works.

This book emerged in part because of a silly fight over the meaning of the word 'elite', which has become one of those catch-all terms used by reactionaries as a means of cajoling the lower classes into a culture war. This strategy works because there is resentment out there—I've felt it most of my life—but not for the reasons those who wield it would have us believe.

There is a palpable sensation that the elites, conservative commentators included, are sniggering at us behind our backs while we suffer degradations of health, education and economic policy. I say we, but by any standard I am now a middle-class man in the body of a poor boy, with a mind in both homes. The mendacity of the reactionaries is in the simple truth that this is all a performance, for them.

The right-leaning big-talkers are as well read and fed and housed as the most liberal academics in the universities. Largely, their concerns about the working class and, when it suits, the poor are proportionate to the leverage they can pry from these people in a theatre of debate that will never include its subjects. The hard left does it too, and my friends from either side of the political spectrum are frequently guilty of seeing those beneath them as scarcely human but useful rhetorical devices. They are the great uncounted who can be marshalled by any speaker clever enough to suddenly, and en masse, provide ballast for an idea.

All the while I see my mother Deb, who fits precisely into no single set of party values. If left alone in a room with a Greens voter, Labor one, moderate and conservative Liberal voter, she would spend a great deal of time figuring out how to escape. It's not because she doesn't care about politics. It's because her trust has been abused by all of the aforementioned at one stage or another.

At the 2016 federal election, Pauline Hanson's One Nation party scored the second-place vote in almost every booth in my mum's electorate of Wright. One Nation beat the Labor Party in Boonah, Aratula, Peak Crossing, Harrisville and Kalbar. The neighbouring federal electorate of Lockyer recorded the highest One Nation vote in the country and, in the 2017 Queensland election, more than one-third of voters in the state seat of the same name opted for Hanson's candidate. The party picked up a mid-north Queensland seat on preference flows.

So what?

The Hanson political machine has risen and fallen before, in almost identical circumstances to those it finds itself in today. A persecution complex meets an ideological pyramid scheme, and voters are grist for the mill. Hanson, like those other great reactionary grifters, has assumed the mantle of outsider even though it fits loosely. Her policies fit the flock she claims to represent even less perfectly. But in those moments when I can inhabit the lives of those in my childhood, I understand the compulsion to try another option. The role of outsider is coveted political ground because that is how the country as a modern democracy began, hidden in the backwaters of the globe.

When Captain Arthur Phillip arrived on the First Fleet in 1788, he carried among the ships a collection of prickly pear cuttings, taken from Brazil, in the hopes of setting up a dye industry to rival that of the Spanish. The Aztecs and Mayan people had discovered that drying out and crushing cochineal insects, which feed on the cactus pads, turned them into the greatest colour red the world had ever seen. The dye was crucial to the British Empire because its emissaries' coats were very, very red and Australia, where officers had been sent to guard a criminal class, was very, very far from home.

The island continent was nothing like the Mother Land at all. This was largely owing to the fact it had been occupied for at least 65 000 years by Aboriginal people and not, say, the British. The animals were weird and at least one of them, the platypus, appeared to be a fake. For the longest time, as the historian and author Robert Hughes noted in his great work *The Fatal Shore*, colonial watercolourists just couldn't draw eucalyptus trees properly. No matter how hard they tried, the gums kept looking like oaks and elms. Indeed, this new place could do with a little sprucing up. And who better to do that than the redcoats?

Despite continued efforts to import the familiarity of home, there was still something about this fledgling colonial outpost that bothered the interlopers: How, if at all, could you tell a gentleman from a working-class man? This society, like the one from which the colonists came, needed the practical distinction of class about as much as it needed the rabbit, or tuberculosis. Nevertheless, a version of class is what they got.

In the modern sense, class is something people worry about when they have the time and resources to do so. Australia's Aboriginal people, who were the first to move onto the continent via land bridges and island hopping in the many tens of millennia before the land saw so much as a bracing cup of tea, had no such class hierarchy. Indigenous tribes were still highly ordered and regulated, but this occurred through the use of complex family structures.

Elders passed on knowledge and culture to those who were younger, and extended families were woven together through routine and custom. Each had their place, though possessions never entered into the equation. It made for an efficient survival mechanism—theirs is the oldest continuing culture alive today.

If history has done its job, we should know by now that it sometimes takes an outsider to do what the group never considered possible. The great novels of fiction and records of antiquity are filled with outsiders who crashed through and plenty who never quite did but lived all the same. Dostoyevsky created one of the first modern outsiders in *Notes from the Underground*. Sartre and Camus perfected the very notion. JD Salinger wrote one of the great literary outsiders in seventeen-year-old Holden Caulfield, who railed against the 'phony' institutions that kept him in check.

Author Neil Griffiths says that to be an outsider is 'to feel disconnected from life, from other people. The sight lines of communication always just slightly skewed. Outsiders can be perceptive readers of inmost thoughts, but they slip off surfaces and are awkward on firm ground. It is their unfortunate role to stand against life.'

There is an education in that stand, however. We come with certain skill sets acquired through necessity and the military college that is struggle. Privilege is the absence of contest, which is no doubt comfortable, but it does not create good citizens. It is a social lethargy that promotes, quite silently, the ignorance of any minority experience.

The writer Rebecca Solnit says 'obliviousness is privilege's form of deprivation' because it makes others 'unreal', only to leave the privileged in a wasteland of a world with just themselves in it. In a piece on Donald Trump, she writes: 'The rich kids I met in college were flailing as though they wanted to find walls around them, leapt as though they wanted there to be gravity and to hit ground, even bottom, but parents and privilege kept throwing out safety nets and buffers, kept padding the walls and picking up the pieces, so that all their acts were meaningless, literally inconsequential. They floated like astronauts in outer space.'

Consequence. In our lives, there was always so much consequence. Every day could make or shatter a future. Several decisions could do it on particularly stressful days.

I've no desire to romanticise our lives, or those of people who have it even worse. For many there is no time for the pride of consequence in their existence. Every day the battlefield is reset. Many do not make it clear of the struggle to see, from a distance, what they might have gained from it.

And what they might have gained from it is this. Meaning.

Even the smallest success means more because it was made in effort. Solnit talks about privilege as if it were a choose-your-own-adventure book where the reader gets to flick ahead and find the option that works best for the story. There are no dead-ends or obstacles, just the smooth world of choices rendered meaningless by circumstance. Taken in this way, the story means little.

The romantic poets struggled with the concept of the sublime. Emily Dickinson saw it as a place where the 'soul should stand in awe' and William Blake called it a 'fearful mystery'. It is a difficult concept to pin down but the poets viewed the sublime as a combination of natural awe and terror, something so grand that it underscored the pointlessness of human endeavour in a messy and dangerous universe.

These natural forces weren't conceived as extending to the systems created by men, but they ought to have been. What is anyone to do when up against the forces of inequality and class, family breakdown and the erosion of love as a unifying force? Now there is awe and terror. In this way, the easier pleasures of existence mean less and the difficult ones are more worthy. It is of little consolation to my mum, who has never freed herself from this involuntary parade of difficulty, but in those desperate hours I have tried to remind her what this sacrifice has created.

'The stories we have, people just wouldn't believe them,' she has told me throughout the years. 'They don't believe that there are people out there like the Mortons, people who can do what they did to their own family.' There is a tendency in this country to spurn hard-luck stories. My friend Michael has reduced this to a pithy one-liner: yeah, we've all got stuff going on, mate. It is a humorous veneer across the surface of a deeper thought crime: to meditate at length on the forces that keep any of us in place. And yet to do otherwise is to give succour to those same forces, animated from above by the ruling classes.

Taken in isolation, any one of these forces may seem insignificant, like a tumbleweed. The barren plains of my childhood home are filled with tumbleweeds. They're actually several species of plant with one thing in common: at maturity they die off and detach from the root system and go on a cross-country adventure. The weeds grow in almost perfect balls and are so light and brittle they can be carried vast distances by the wind, all the while bouncing seeds out onto the ground as they go. A single tumbleweed does nothing but spin and move.

Collectively, however, tumbleweeds gather together in spindly stretches as long as the horizon and can bring down fences as if they had never even been there. This is the power of the singular and weak and a handy reminder of what those small indentations can do to minds and bodies over time.

The Australian author Steve Toltz calls the past 'an inoperable tumour that spreads to the present'. I've long struggled with the fatalism that lives in that statement. There can be no doubt about its fundamental truth—if only because time's arrow runs in one direction and we build the past to get where it is pointing—but it doesn't have to be terminal.

It has been more than two decades since my immediate family imploded. So much of the intervening years, personally, has been a curious mix of joy and the overwhelming isolation of having survived something that cannot be put into words. The joy, the joy is easy. Every step towards independence and capacity has knocked down one of the walls I put up to protect myself.

In Year 12, because I was in search of something different, me and three friends opened a computer store in Boonah. By the time I'd told Mum what we were doing I'd paid the first month's rent ($550) on a shopfront, while in my school uniform, and established a relationship with several wholesalers and a courier company. Mum flipped her lid, and with good reason. I mean, it was a remarkably stupid idea. There were already two other computer stores in town run by actual businesspeople. Only one of us had a licence so he became our call-out computer technician. Another member of the laughably loose 'partnership' was a 23-year-old stoner who had a penchant for not turning up on time to open the store during school hours.

We mostly used the store as an excuse to play networked computer games late at night. I lived a five-minute walk down the road and would occasionally enlist the help of a mate to lug my desktop computer and screen to the store and back when we didn't have enough computers to play. Late one night, while we were struggling home with the computer equipment, the local cops pulled over and asked if we were up to anything in particular. I imagine our response was incredibly disappointing.

The joy was trying sushi for the first time on my maiden trip to Sydney when my well-travelled friend Joe Corrigan and I got into a screaming match because I didn't want to put the raw salmon in my mouth and he wouldn't rest until I did. It was amazing.

In many ways I think I needed to become a journalist because I knew reporting would teach me about the world I'd been denied as a kid. I might have made more money in law but it would have afforded me precious little in the way of excuses to become involved.

The single best day I've had in my job was in late 2015 when I flew into Griffith and drove three hours west to spend a day with the Ngiyampaa Wangaaypuwan people, just as Mawonga Station was about to be handed back to them. We climbed to the top of a ridge in the open countryside, through the beech trees and dogwood plants, and peered in on ancient rock art and old millstone sites where Aboriginal people ground local seeds to use as aphrodisiacs. The elders told me stories about how they used to take fruit from local farmers, watermelons and all, and throw them into the river so they could walk past the landholders with empty hands, then they'd collect the fruit downstream.

The peculiar ripples of anxiety for an outsider are salved somewhat by days like that. Anxiety that I haven't done enough, read enough, heard enough. Trauma, like a comet, has a long tail and I have spent my life running to keep in front of it.

It never occurred to me that people, like the self-styled prophets of the everyman in the commentariat, could elect to become an outsider. To be so closed off from the world is not to come close to power and be rebuffed by it. It is a feeling, dragged with you from childhood, that drips through the body like phlegm. This state of otherness is to be trapped in a perspex box in the middle of a crowded thoroughfare. You can see the people milling about, attending to their lives in a thousand different ways, but you cannot reach them. Observation is key but belonging is not an option.

You might be forgiven for thinking this is all about money. That's what poverty means, right? And it's true. For all the patronising axioms about money never buying happiness, it does allow for other things that help. It buys time to spend with families, mobility, the uniquely preservative state of having a home to sleep in and knowing that you always will. It can pay for one, two or even nine attempts at drug rehab for your brother if that is what it takes.

That's why class warfare is such an odious term. It invokes the myth of equality to enlist those who might benefit from a clinical discussion into a pseudo-fight for their place on the ladder. The danger always comes from below and there are always those poorer and more hopelessly resourced underfoot who might constitute a threat. And beneath them? More. It's turtles all the way down. The trick is in the distraction.

But there is a poverty of culture and access, too. A surplus of the kind of stress that devours from within and eventually damages rationality for good. And there is a poverty of love.

The writer Mary Gaitskill makes a living exploring the 'chambers of the heart' that few of us ever gain access to. A revealing profile of the author in *The New York Times Magazine* by Paul Sehgal shows us her monsters are not the classics of horror but the ones that come from within. 'Gaitskill's fiction unfolds in these psychological spaces; she knows that we, unlike plants, don't always grow toward the light, that sometimes we cannot even be coaxed toward it,' Sehgal writes.

Part of my diminished childhood was on account of one person who ought to have been able to love me and my brother and sister the way he wanted to, but was, for reasons to do with his own beginnings, entirely unable to. Our father, at least for us, could not be coaxed towards the light.

He stopped writing birthday cards to Lauryn when she turned four. Dad had known her for all of three weeks when he pushed the ejector button. He didn't see her again until she reached her twenties, and since then scarcely at all. As for Toby and I, for a while we visited him every other school holiday. For that reason, I will never again get on a McCafferty's bus so long as I am alive, an ambition helped along by the fact they merged with Greyhound in 2004. The trip, depending on what station Dad was managing at the time, could take in excess of twenty hours. I took packets of Chico babies for sustenance and a little pillow you could blow air into. The best roadhouse for food was always at Augathella in Queensland's far west.

My brother and I were both still in primary school when we made one trip to Tranby Station, via Winton in the state's central-west. Mum and I had agreed on a code phrase before we left. If I was unhappy or something had gone wrong, I just had to tell her 'the horses are pretty lovely' over the phone. I'm not sure what would have happened next. Those plans are for adults and Mum was doing her best to shield me from having to be an adult.

One night during that break, Dad drove us over to a neighbour's house where he drank himself into a stupor. Toby drove us home along a stretch of highway past road trains while Dad vomited out the passenger window. I thought it was hilarious. Mum did not.

Because the bus trips were unbearable, at the next holidays Dad suggested we fly out because it would be easier, but then he refused to pay for the $800 return fares. Mum asked her own mother for a loan and paid instead, so that we might have more time to spend with Dad.

I haven't spoken with Dad in almost a decade now. We are Facebook friends though, for what it's worth. He messaged 'happy bday Rick' on two occasions and once, curiously, liked a post I had written about how the agrarian revolution was a mistake that mankind, if it knew what it was getting itself into, would never have made willingly. We are like rocks skipping across a body of water we call time. Each of us carries the energy of the past into the next generation. The slightest perturbations in the throw are magnified and become harder to correct in each subsequent jump. Yet we go on. We work at it.

In the lead-up to Christmas in 2017 I spent eleven days driving through outback Queensland from Longreach through Winton, Barcaldine, Tambo, Windorah and on to Birdsville. It is quite bizarre to return to a part of the country where everybody knows a piece of the Morton story. Every other person knows my father—had cattle on agistment with him, worked with him—and everyone knew my grandfather George. But there was only one character that counted, to my eyes, and that was the emptiness itself.

Australian film often makes the outback the leading actor and you have to breathe it in yourself to understand why. It's what the poets meant when they talked about the sublime. And it is mine. I might not belong with the people there any more than I belong to the ones in the city, but the red earth is mine. If you stop on the side of the road between two far-flung towns at night and turn off the lights, the evening sky rushes in at you. Light pollution scars the view in the city but out there the access is unfettered. A single man becomes an elite; the sky is his, too.

I remember once sleeping out under the same stars on Mount Howitt Station, on a trampoline, nestled into the crook of my father's arm. We traced the Southern Cross and I completely failed to see the Big Dipper. Memory is such a cocktail and I have no way of knowing the truth of this, but that felt like the happiest night of my life for so long.

I collected imitations of that love for years, and bundled friends and mentors and great affections into that particular void for decades. Our poverty, in the end, was one I don't have an answer for.

Of course, I still love Dad, but I don't know why. It is cruel to think that shall remain while the work at loving myself and rebuilding my own confidence continues. The surest thing about my life has always been Mum, the woman who held the earth together like those great cap-rock ranges outside Winton. She is the hero of this piece and she looms in my mind as large and unchanging as the monumental vistas out west.

'I didn't do anything, you got yourself out,' she told me on the phone while I was writing this book. She, this woman of faith, is an atheist when it comes to her own work. She sees wonder and splendour and hope and no hand of the maker involved. But of course it was Mum who steadied me and then set my life in motion. What feels like eons have passed now and I wonder if she could have known the outcome of her alien mythology: boy enters world, mother sees boy as special, tells him he was sent here from that big night sky by beings unknown to report back on what he sees. She invented the aliens because she couldn't see herself as the protagonist. She outsourced the explanation for her own success as a mother to the aliens out there. And here we are—I'm ready to reveal my findings.

It was her. It was always Deb.

What could have been different? Everything and nothing. What should have been different? Not us. We did the best we could with what we had. There is beauty in that, the way you can find beauty in imperfection. I could never have predicted this life for myself. The dreams get bigger, the joy more profound, the reminders of the past less potent.

From the age of eight I promised Mum that one day I would build a granny flat for her to live in. Recently, I told her I should quite like to live in New York one day.

'Oh, you're not going to live in a loft are you?' she asked.

'You can have the apartment next door,' I told her.

I don't know precisely how I'm going to do this but, on balance, I've never known how I was going to do anything. Luck feels like the wrong word. Stochasticity seems better. All I know is that I feel governed by time, perhaps no more or less than the average person, but keenly nonetheless. There is a sense of urgency to make up for my years in the wilderness.

There is always time for wonder.

In a large escarpment outside of Birdsville there are some dingo caves where a person can stand, as I have, and survey the empire of dirt first established by my great-grandfather Celsus Morton. Facing in one direction, everything that fits into my field of vision is still in the hands of my extended family. It is an impossible amount of space coated like rust by gibber rocks. Imagine a burnt-red mirror laid across the 10 625 square kilometres that made up the old Roseberth Station (before it was cleaved in two) and then see it shatter into billions of pieces over the landscape. That's the gibber rocks. They seem to change colour as the sun moves across the sky. The direct light of midday gives the rocks a deep purple hue but as the sun's rays become angular in the late afternoon, the rust colour really begins to pop. From this vantage point, as far as the eye can see, the property seems like the surface of Mars. You can almost picture the scientists roaming across the surface and pointing out the telltale signs of where water once flowed but hasn't for millennia.

It is easy, under such conditions, to find yourself wondering how anything at all can grow out here. Though of course you know that things do.

Acknowledgements

It takes a village to raise a child, perhaps two to produce an author.

This book is the product of a lifetime of fine grace and support from wonderful and clever people. Thanks to my earliest teachers, Marcia Wimmer and Moya Rabbitt, who helped me grip the English language, to Bob Gray and Kathy Neuendorf, who nurtured my curiosity, and those later in life, Roxane Scott and Jackie Campbell, who taught me how to wring meaning out of the tiniest spaces.

There is so much gratitude to my first boss, Wendy Creighton, who gave me extra jobs for extra money in those lean high-school years, even when it meant irrevocably destroying the paint on her office ceiling. And thanks again for taking me in as a wee journalist with nowhere to go.

I have met and come to know true giants. To my closest and wisest friend, Bridie Jabour, thank you for propping me up and alternately protecting and gently mocking my fragile sense of self. To all the Jabours and an errant Boyle, thank you for taking me in.

Seamus, a thousand times yes. Alice, you get me. Anna, flatmate, come back. Matty Q, I want to be you.

My favourite Slav, Sabina Husic, has plied me with Negronis and cheer. And to Shannon Molloy, that gorgeous friend and human everyone deserves to have in their life, I am lucky to have you.

Monica, your mad stories and your irrepressible joy have sustained me. Gratitude to my longest-serving friends, Tyson and Sam Harvey, Matthew Collyer and his brother David, Latham Barnes and Steph Kerr. To Tony and Yvette Barnes, too, thanks for taking me on those summer camping trips to play board games. Britteny, I am sorry about Year 9.

In the throes of extreme self-doubt, the early readers of this book set my mind at ease. Shaun Crowe provided advice down to the comma and Tom Rabe made meticulous notes. Thank you, too, to the wise and measured Eric George for his counsel, and the powerful troika of Emily Ritchie, Simone Fox Koob and Sam Buckingham-Jones for their support. Nicholas Adams-Dzierzba provided big-picture thinking.

My joy-soaked thanks go to the Kilby boys, who put me up while I wrote some of this. Dan, Jayden, Jack, Aidan and Tom, my head still hurts. Same to you, too, Derrick Krusche.

And, of course, where would I be without Michael Roddan. My mate Mike heard about the project at every turn and has even helped, on the odd occasion. Thank you to the rest of my colleagues, especially the mighty Sydney bureau and my dear friend Stephen Fitzpatrick. Gemma, the beanie helped. Sam Leckie, Mum is lucky to have you. SJ Tasker and Sandy Bresic pumped me up when I needed to hear it. Mitchy Bingemann, thanks for encouraging me to write more. Father Peter Gablonski, we need more helpful and compassionate people like you in the world.

Sammy Cochrane, you complete me and helped me complete this. Lana Hirschowitz, thank you for taking a chance on me— and three times since, just in the making of this book. Clive Mathieson, I'm glad I get to call you a friend. You backed me when it counted most. And to Hamish, whom I adore. I'm sorry your own mother forgot to name you in her book.

To my own family, especially Deb and Lauryn, look what we did. I'm so proud.